INTRODUCTION, THE A4D-3:

INTRODUCTION, THE A4D-3: In the Navy's neverending quest to improve a good thing, the A4D-3 proposal was drafted in February 1957 to update the A4D-2 to a limited all-weather light attack aircraft. In addition, it was to have increased range and a more powerful J65-W-10 engine of 8,500lbs, later switched to a J52-P-4 engine of 7,850lbs but weighing 600lbs less.

Other improvements were:
+ **Fixed cambered leading edge.**
+ **Improved elevator effectiveness at high speeds.**
+ **TACAN**
+ **Ranging radar (AN/APG-53).**
+ **Aero 26A or Mk. 9 weapon sights.**
+ **Three-axis autopilot with automatic LABS.**
+ **Improved catapult and landing gear strength.**

A contract was signed on 14 February for four aircraft, but fiscal concerns intervened and the project was cancelled.

THE A4D-2N/A-4C: In September 1957, the Navy allowed Douglas to pursue a limited all-weather fix for the Skyhawk. This became the A4D-2N or A-4C in 1962. The AN/APG-53A from the A4D-3 proposal was installed as was an AN/AJB-3 all-attitude flight reference and bombing system, an automatic flight control system, and an improved AN/ASN-19A navigation computer.

The avionics changes required a major re-alignment of the cockpit. The principal problem was to find room for the 5-inch square AJB-3 display. The armament panel was moved downward and the instruments and controls were rearranged on the instrument panel.

The aircraft's structure changed about 15%, which included the nose

Above, the first A4D-2N, BuNo 145062, made its first flight on 21 August 1958. Bob Drew was the test pilot. Externally, the A4D-2N differed from the A4D-2 in having a 9-inch longer nose and refueling probe and a black radome. (Harry Gann) Bottom, artist's drawing of the canceled A4D-3 proposal. Four aircraft were ordered, BuNos 145147-145150, but all were canceled. (Harry Gann)

and refueling probe to be stretched 9-inches. Although the J52 was planned, the A-4C ended up with a J65-W-20 engine of 8,300lbs thrust and an overall empty weight of

9,728lbs.

Initially, besides the lengthened nose, the A4D-2N could easily be discerned by its black radome. This design was changed to a paintable dielectric material with a white or black erosion-resistant area on the tip of the nose. These were retrofitted to all A4D-2Ns as were windshield wipers on or about the same time. Also during production, the 5 liter liquid oxygen system was replaced with a 10 liter unit and the engine oil capacity also was increased.

The A4D-2N was equipped with a Douglas Escapac I ejection seat that provided for a ground level ejection at speeds above 90 knots. Its sides were extended upwards and fowards, the seat support system and inertia reel were improved, and a safety was added to the front of the headrest. The units also were retrofit-

ted to all A4D-1 and A4D-2 Skyhawks.

Although I would classify the A4D-2N/A-4C an interim design in the Skyhawk series, it was the most prolific with 638 airframes produced. These were BuNos 145062-145146, 147669-147849, 148304-148317, 148435-148612, 149487-149646, 150581-150600.

The first flight of the A4D-2N was made by Bob Drew on 21 August 1958 in BuNo 145062. Bob would make the first flight on the first nine A4D-2Ns, BuNos 145062-145071. The first flight of the second A4D-2N, BuNo 145063, was made by Drew on 17 November 1958.

THE A-4L: At the start of the Vietnam War, the Naval Reserve was operating a vast fleet of A-4A/B Skyhawks. As the war progressed, A-4Cs found

Above, the second A4D-2N, BuNo 145063, at Douglas on 31 October 1958 with da-glo red nose, intake, outer wing and vertical tail trim. (Harry Gann) Bottom, BuNo 145063 viewed from the right side. Note the red stripes on the gear doors and speed brake. (Harry Gann)

their way to the reserves as they were replaced with more capable A-4E/Fs and A-7A/Bs. But these aircraft were no longer compatible with the fleet because they lacked the tactical and defensive electronic equipment found in fleet aircraft over Vietnam. In 1970, the Navy reorganized the reserves into two deployable carrier air wings that needed to be equipped with upgraded aircraft. The solution for the attack squadrons was to upgrade the A-4C with electronic and hardware

changes that would emulate the A-4F. The J65 engine and the three external stores pylons were not changed, but the fuselage hump found on most A-4Fs was added to the A-4Cs to house the new avionics. Another addition was the installation of lift spoilers to the wings.

Douglas modified one A-4C, BuNo 148307, into the first A-4L. Its first flight was conducted on 21 August 1969. The reserves then received 99 conversion kits which were installed at the Naval Air Rework Facilities (NARFs). The 100 A-4Ls were BuNos 145065, 145076-145078, 145092, 145101, 145103, 145114, 145117, 145119, 145121-145122, 145128, 145133, 145141, 147669, 147671, 147690, 147703, 147706, 147708, 147717, 147723, 147727, 147736, 147750, 147754, 147761, 147768, 147772, 147780, 147782, 147787, 147793, 147796, 147798, 147802, 147807, 147815, 147825, 147827, 147836, 147843, 148306, 148307, 148316, 148436, 148446, 148453, 148479, 148487, 148490, 148498, 148505, 148530, 148538, 148555, 148578, 148581, 148586, 148588, 148600, 148602, 148611, 149497, 149500, 149502, 149506, 149508, 149516, 149518, 149531, 149532, 149536, 149539, 149540, 149551, 149555, 149556, 149569, 149573, 149579, 149583, 149591, 149593, 149595, 149604, 149607, 149608, 149620, 149623, 149626, 149630, 149633, 149635, 149640, 149646, 150586, 150593, and 150598.

As these A-4Ls were replaced with A-4E/Fs and A-7A/Bs in the reserves, many were then acquired by the utility VC squadrons.

A-4C/A-4L LEADING PARTICULARS

FUSELAGE:

Length	42 ft. 10-7/8 in.
Length on the Fuselage Reference Line Level	41 ft. 7-1/4 in.
Height	14 ft. 11-7/8 in.
Height on the Fuselage Reference Line Level	18 ft. 3-3/8 in.
Height in Hoisting Attitude	15 ft. 8-5/8 in.
Width Maximum	5 ft. 4 in.
Ground Angle Fus. Reference Line to Static Ground Line	5 deg. 59 min.
Angle Between Fus. Ref. Line and Wing Zero Lift Line	0°

WING:

Span	27 ft. 6 in.
Airfoil Section at Root	NACA 0.0008-1. 1-25-0.0875 (0.5x230)
Airfoil Section at Theoretical Tip	NACA 0.0005-0. 825-50-0.0787 (0.5x230)
Chord at Root Section	15 ft. 6 in.
Chord at Construction Tip	3 ft. 6 in.
Mean Aerodynamic Chord	10 ft. 9-5/8 in.
Dihedral	2 deg. 41 min.
Incidence	0°
Sweepback at 25% Chord	33 deg. 12 min
Aspect Ratio	2.91

HORIZONTAL STABILIZER:

Span Including Elevators	11 ft. 8 in.
Maximum Chord at Station 0	6 ft. 8 in.
Dihedral	0°
Incidence Normal	0°
Incidence Adjustment	11° up 1° down

AREAS:

Wings Including Ailerons, Flaps and 60.8 sq. ft, of Fus.	259.82 sq. ft.
Ailerons Including 0.5 sq. ft. of Trim Tab Area	16.33 sq. ft.
Flaps	22.25 sq. ft.
Spoilers	24 sq. ft.
Horizontal Stabilizer Including Elevators	46.54 sq. ft.
Elevators	11.33 sq. ft.
Vertical Fin Less Rudder	41.03 sq. ft.
Rudder	9.21 sq. ft.

LANDING GEAR:

Main Gear Wheel Tread	7 ft. 9-1/2 in.
Main Gear Wheel Base	11 ft. 11-1/8 in.
Arresting Hook Travel	64°

WEIGHTS:

Normal Gross Weight	16,046 lbs.
Gross Weight Reworked Per A-4 AFC 278	16,082 lbs.
Gross Weight Reworked Per A-4 AFC 325-I through -XI	16,174
Complete Aircraft Empty	9,440 lbs.
Complete Aircraft Empty with AFC 278	9,476 lbs.
Complete Aircraft Empty with AFC 325-I through -XI	9,568 lbs.
(Add 40 lbs. to the Above Weights for J65-W-20 in the A-4L)	
Designed Gross Weight of Aircraft (Catapult)	19,910 lbs.
Complete Aircraft Empty A-4L	10,319 lbs.
Fuselage Forward Section	2,394 lbs.
Fuselage Forward Section with AFC 278	2,430 lbs.
Fuselage Forward Section with AFC 325-I through -XI	2,512 lbs.
Fuselage Forward Section A-4L	2,846 lbs.
Fuselage Aft Section	1,937 lbs.
Fuselage Aft Section with AFC 325-I through -XI	1,947 lbs.
Approach Power Compensator with AFC 278	36 lbs.
Generator A-4L	52 lbs.
Voltage Regulator AFC 325-I through -XI	3 lbs.
Spoilers A-4L	21.5 lbs.
AN/APG-53A Radar	51 lbs.
AN/ASQ-17B	122 lbs.
In-Flight refueling Store Dry	700 lbs.
Aero 1C 150 Gallon Drop Tanks	132 lbs.
Aero 1C 300 Gallon Drop Tanks	200 lbs.

A4D-2N SKYHAWK FLIGHT REPORT BY C. H. MEYER DATED 1 JULY 1960

On 17 June 1960, the writer flew two production delivery A4D-2N Skyhawks for a total time of three hours. The first was flown with two 300 gallon tanks, and the second was flown in the clean configuration.

SUMMARY: Although this airplane was originally designed to be a light-weight simple follow-on for the AD Skyraider series, it has since grown to be very capable, moderately sophisticated weapons system that is currently being developed in large production numbers to have exceptionally good day and night low altitude, close air support and interdiction capabilities for the following reasons:

1.) This airplane is extremely easy to fly. Both systems checkout and flight characteristics would make it easy to train low-time pilots just out of operational training.
2.) The A4D-2N can make catapult and arrested landings with zero wind over the deck in its long-range tactical configuration.
3.) The airplane has designed 7G ground attack strength. At the present time, the structural demonstration is not complete and it is limited to 6G.
4.) Performance wise the airplane shows a true level flight high speed of .92 in the clean configuration, and a .875 V-max with two 300 gallon tanks. Time-to-climb is good to 35,000 feet in the heaviest weight tested, and the airplane shows an average long-range cruise altitude of 30,000-to-35,000 feet.
5.) This weapons system is developing an excellent maintenance record (FIP 8.2 direct maintenance hours/flight hour).
6.) There is sufficient growth potential in the airplane to make it useful in fleet operations for the next 5-to-8 years.

WEAPONS SYSTEM: In the writer's opinion this weapons system has the possibility of becoming asymptotic to an all-weather weapons system as any small, light-weight aircraft can. By virtue of the development of the following systems and state of the art, and with the high-level practice by squadron personnel, this airplane might possibly approach an all-weather aircraft except for delivery of stores.

1.) AUTOMATIC FLIGHT CONTROL SYSTEM: This system is made by Eclipse Pioneer for the A4D-2N only. It is completely transistorized and weighs only 90lbs complete. This system has a capability of maintaining heading, altitude, attitude, coordinating turns to a pre-selected heading, maneuvering with the normal pilot operated stick, yaw damping and ground control bombing. Ground control bombing (TPQ-10) is a system whereby a ground controller can direct the airplane in roll and yaw including release of weapons. The pilot flies the pitch control.

The writer used the AFCS continuously through the entire flight in all of the modes and was most impressed with it because the general natural stability level of the airplane is so low that the automatic pilot is required to do an exceptionally good job of flying the airplane. The writer could find no crabs in the AFCS. The ground control bombing system is not yet operational but is in the experimental testing stages.

2.) ASN-19A NAVIGATION COMPUTER: This system is built by Bendix, weighs 25lbs (plus the compass and the air speed computer) and has a test stand tolerance of 12 miles. It is designed only to get the airplane back to within TACAN range of the carrier and it will do this to the satisfaction of the Navy. This system can have variation and wind correction cranked in manually. It can not only take the airplane to the target, but also has a memory circuit to return it to home base even with offset doglegs to the ground, specifically hot enemy territory, storms, etc. The writer used this system on an hour and 50 minute flight which included high and low level flight, LABs maneuvers, etc., and although no wind was cranked in, there was only an error of 27 miles at the end of the flight.

3.) APG-53A RADAR: This system weighs 72lbs, is 85% transistorized and made by NAFI and Stewart-Warner. This system has mapping, plan and elevation terrain clearance, and ranging through the visual gunsight. The terrain clearance mode has 1,000 feet reference line below the airplane on the indicater and although the presentation does not seem straightforward in the beginning, is not difficult to become used to. This 7 kw system can search out to 40 miles, has a plus or minus 30° azimuth, 15 inch antenna, and costs $10,000 in production. This system has a range potential to 20,000 yards, but is presently only adjusted for a range as far as 12,000 yards.

4.) AJB-3 LAB SYSTEM: This Lear system has a good, clear, 5-inch, all attitude presentation, is non-gimbaling, weighs 20lbs and has excellent presentation for LABs maneuvers. This system also coordinates the AFCS for turns and works the directional gyro. The one error in the system is that there is no back-up gyro in the airplane, and if the gyro fails, the standby compass is the only alternate. Douglas realizes this error and is planning a back-up gyro.

5.) The present airplane has two wing racks (1,200lbs each) and the centerline rack (3,575lbs). All variety of bombs, rockets, etc., are capable of being carried and the airplane also has the complete ASM-N-7 Bullpup system installed with a special maneuvering control on the stick grip for the Bullpup weapon. Armament consists of two Mk. 12, MOD O, 20mm guns with 1,000 rounds of ammunition each. The airplane is provisioned to carry AN/AWW-1 special store delivery equipment.

6.) AIRCRAFT COMMUNICATIONS, NAVIGATION: Equipment includes ARA-25, ARN-21 TACAN. ARN-14E and ARR-12 beacons are carried in the navigation pack on the centerline station of the airplane for stateside navigation.

7.) The present airplane is equipped with a very simple, Douglas designed rocket-powered sea level ejection seat that is good for ejection about 90 knots on the ground. The seat is being further developed so that it will be safe for ejection down to 30 knots.

MISSION CAPABILITY: A summary of mission capabilities is as follows in the standard high-low-high type of mission.

CONFIGURATION	ALTITUDE	RADIUS
Long-Range Attack Radius (two 300 gallon tanks, one TX-28)	29,000 feet to 34,000 feet	650 nautical miles
	Sea Level	350 nautical miles
Intermediate Range Attack (two 150 gallon tanks, one TX-28)	32,000 feet to 34,000 feet	575 nautical miles
	Sea Level	300 nautical miles
Basic Attack (three Bullpups)	34,000 feet to 36,000 feet	390 nautical miles
	Sea Level	200 nautical miles
Clean	36,000 feet to 38,000 feet	460 nautical miles
	Sea Level	200 nautical miles

The A4D-2N is designed to be able to take off and cruise in inclement weather to within 2,000 feet of terrain, do visual bombing day or night, return in inclement weather and land aboard the carrier in inclement weather.

GENERAL INFORMATION: In service use, the A4D has sustained 9.5 Gs with no damage, 10 Gs with the loss of wing slats. 10.5 Gs is calculated to make the entire airplane disintegrate. There have been no instances of structural failure in the air in the A4D.

A-4C / A-4L INTERNAL STRUCTURES

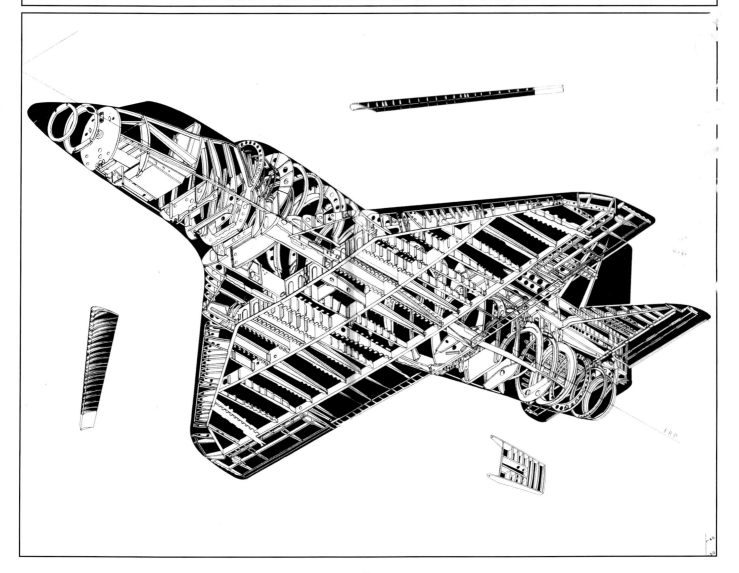

DOUGLAS A-4C SKYHAWK GENERAL ARRANGEMENT

1.) Air Refueling Probe
2.) Radome
3.) Total Temperature Sensor
4.) Brake Fluid Level Window
5.) Pitot Tube
6.) Thermal Radiation Closure
7.) Oxygen Overboard Vent
8.) UHF Radio Antenna
9.) Normal Cockpit Entry Handle
10.) External Canopy-Jettison
11.) 20mm Guns
12.) Angle-Of-Attack Approach Light
13.) Anticollision Lights
14.) Catapult Hooks
15.) External Power Receptacle
16.) Four Hook Ejector Rack
17.) Taxi Light
18.) Missile Guidance Antenna
19.) A-O-A Vane & Transducer
20.) TACAN Antenna
21.) Static Orifice
22.) UHF/ADF Antenna Cover
23.) Nose Com. Access Door
24.) Oil Tank Fillercap
25.) Oil Tank
26.) Fuel Nozzle Ground
27.) Fuel Tank Fillercap
28.) Wing Position Lights
29.) Canopy Air Cylinder
30.) IFF-SIF Radar ID Antenna

31.) AN/ASQ-17
32.) Radar Transmitter/Receiver
33.) Emergency Generator
34.) Fuselage Fuel Tank
35.) Air Refueling Probe Light
36.) Wing Tank Fillercap
37.) Slat
38.) Barricade Engagement Detent
39.) Vortex Generators
40.) Integral Wing Fuel Tank
41.) Arresting Hook
42.) JATO Igniter Terminal
43.) JATO Mounting Hooks
44.) Speedbrake

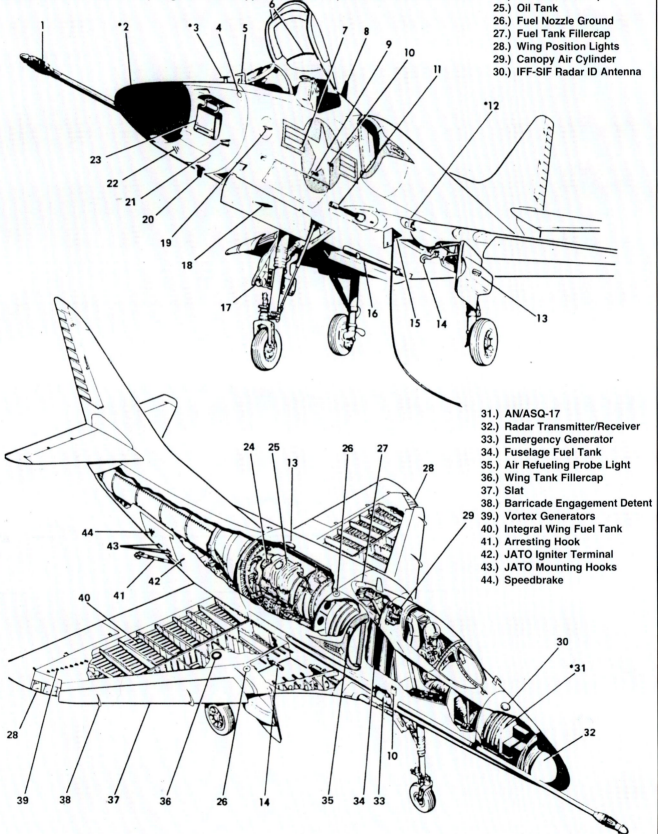

6

DOUGLAS A-4L SKYHAWK GENERAL ARRANGEMENT

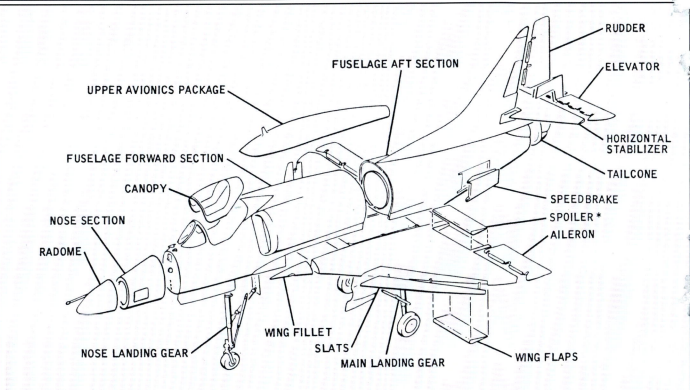

*A-4L ONLY

1.) Inflight Refueling Probe
2.) OA-1906/APG-53A
3.) Nose Radome
4.) Nose Electric Equipment
5.) Rain Removal Nozzle
6.) Gunsight
7.) Rocket Ejection Seat
8.) Cockpit Enclosure Bungee
9.) Fuel Cell Gravity Filler
10.) AB-U-1478 UHF Blade Antenna
11.) Upper Avionics Pod
12.) Engine Oil Tank
13.) Anticollision Light
14.) Rudder Power Mechanism
15.) Horizontal Stabilizer Actuator
16.) Speedbrake
17.) LOX System Overboard Vent
18.) LOX Converter
19.) Spoiler (Flap Beneath)
20.) Wing Integral Fuel Tank

21.) Aileron Followup Trim Tab
22.) Vortex Generators
23.) Navigation Lights
24.) Barricade Strap Detent
25.) Wing Hardpoint
26.) Catapult Hook

27.) Approach Light
28.) 20mm Gun
29.) Canopy External Jettison
30.) Throttle Lever
31.) Angle-Of-Attack Vane & Transducer

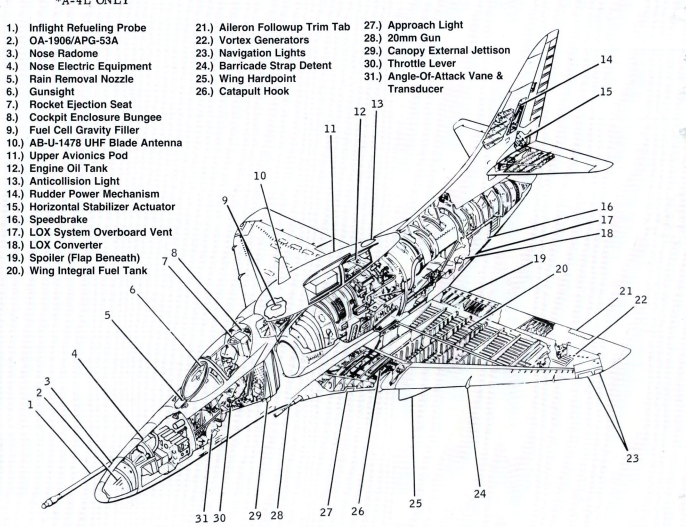

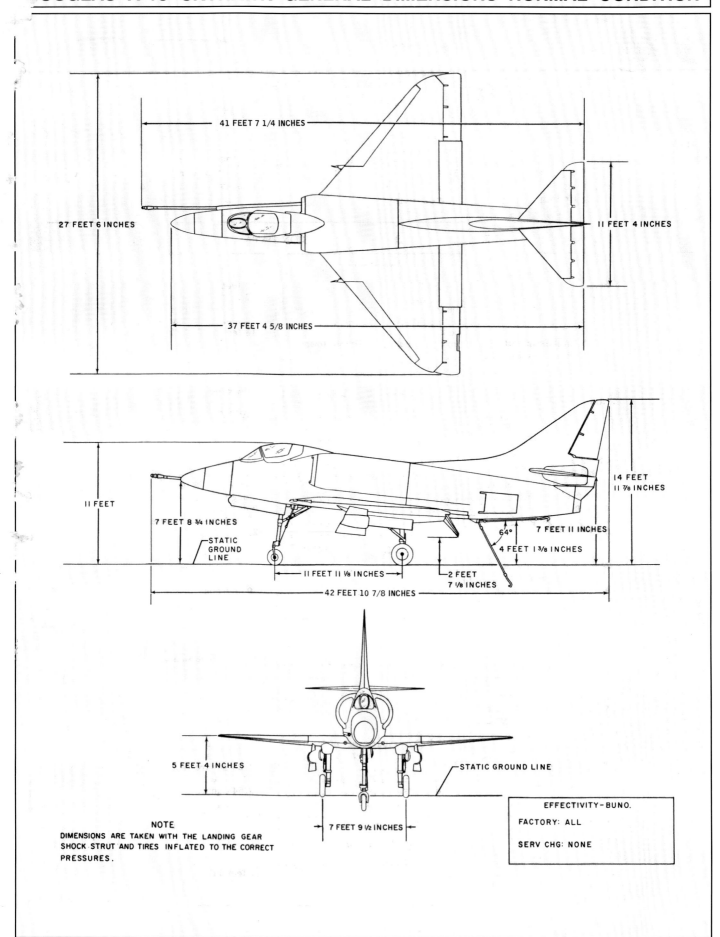

41 FEET 7 1/4 INCHES

27 FEET 6 INCHES

11 FEET 4 INCHES

37 FEET 4 5/8 INCHES

14 FEET 11 7/8 INCHES

11 FEET

7 FEET 8 3/4 INCHES

STATIC GROUND LINE

64°

7 FEET 11 INCHES

4 FEET 1 3/8 INCHES

11 FEET 11 1/8 INCHES

2 FEET 7 1/8 INCHES

42 FEET 10 7/8 INCHES

5 FEET 4 INCHES

STATIC GROUND LINE

7 FEET 9 1/2 INCHES

NOTE
DIMENSIONS ARE TAKEN WITH THE LANDING GEAR SHOCK STRUT AND TIRES INFLATED TO THE CORRECT PRESSURES.

EFFECTIVITY-BUNO.

FACTORY: ALL

SERV CHG: NONE

8

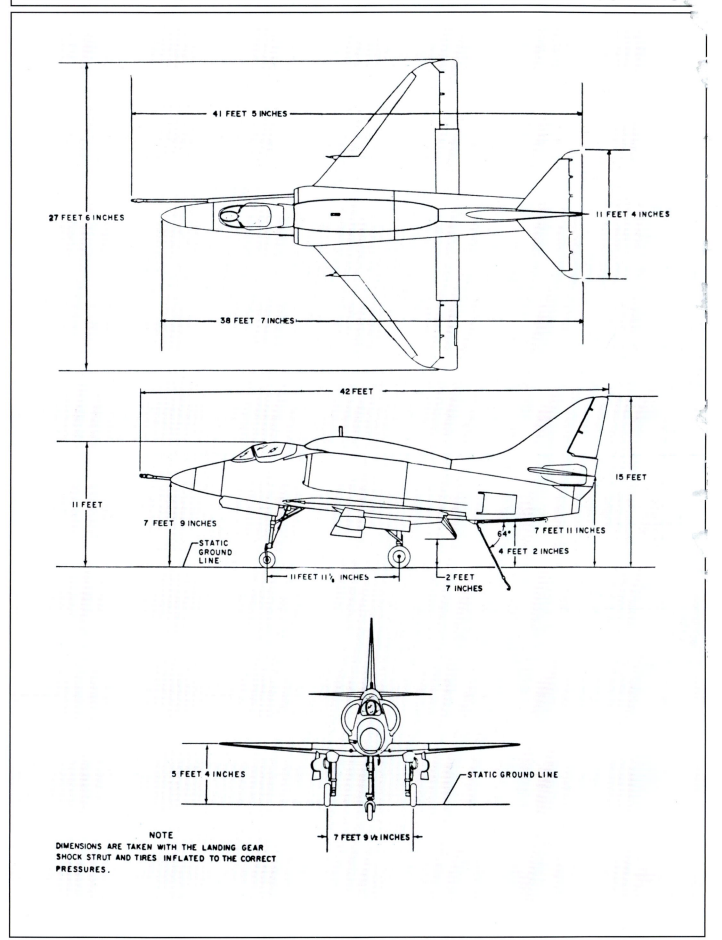

NOTE

DIMENSIONS ARE TAKEN WITH THE LANDING GEAR SHOCK STRUT AND TIRES INFLATED TO THE CORRECT PRESSURES.

ABNORMAL CONDITION DROP TANK CLEARANCES

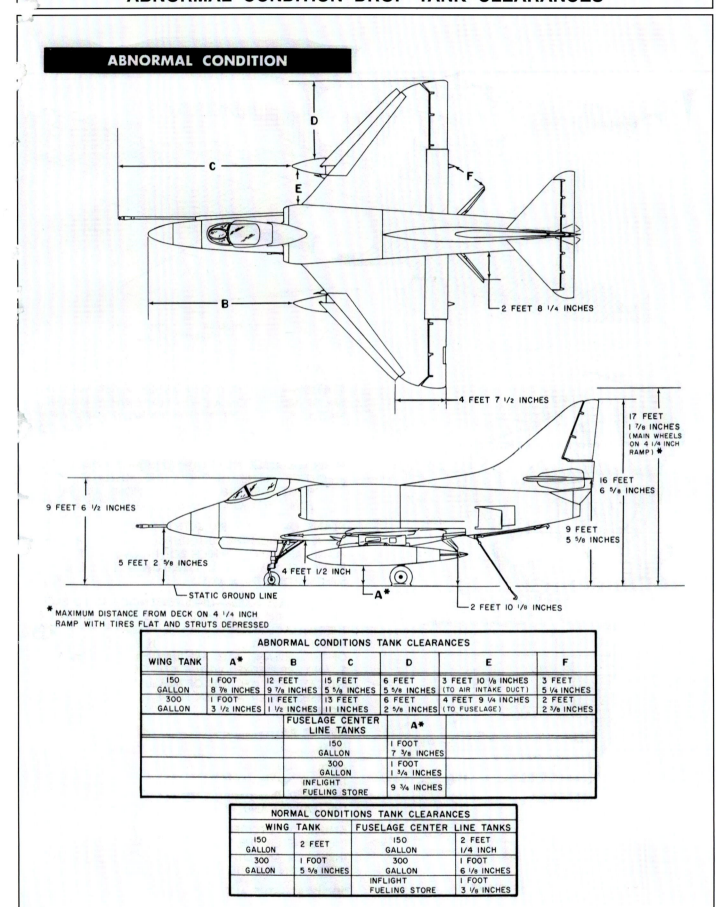

ABNORMAL CONDITION

2 FEET 8 1/4 INCHES

4 FEET 7 1/2 INCHES

17 FEET 1 7/8 INCHES (MAIN WHEELS ON 4 1/4 INCH RAMP) *

16 FEET 6 5/8 INCHES

9 FEET 6 1/2 INCHES

9 FEET 5 5/8 INCHES

5 FEET 2 5/8 INCHES

4 FEET 1/2 INCH

STATIC GROUND LINE

A*

2 FEET 10 1/8 INCHES

* MAXIMUM DISTANCE FROM DECK ON 4 1/4 INCH RAMP WITH TIRES FLAT AND STRUTS DEPRESSED

ABNORMAL CONDITIONS TANK CLEARANCES						
WING TANK	A*	B	C	D	E	F
150 GALLON	I FOOT 8 7/8 INCHES	12 FEET 9 7/8 INCHES	15 FEET 5 5/8 INCHES	6 FEET 5 5/8 INCHES	3 FEET 10 1/8 INCHES (TO AIR INTAKE DUCT)	3 FEET 5 1/4 INCHES
300 GALLON	I FOOT 3 1/2 INCHES	II FEET 1 1/2 INCHES	13 FEET 11 INCHES	6 FEET 2 5/8 INCHES	4 FEET 9 1/4 INCHES (TO FUSELAGE)	2 FEET 2 3/8 INCHES
FUSELAGE CENTER LINE TANKS		A*				
150 GALLON		I FOOT 7 3/8 INCHES				
300 GALLON		I FOOT 1 3/4 INCHES				
INFLIGHT FUELING STORE		9 3/4 INCHES				

NORMAL CONDITIONS TANK CLEARANCES			
WING TANK		FUSELAGE CENTER LINE TANKS	
150 GALLON	2 FEET	150 GALLON	2 FEET 1/4 INCH
300 GALLON	I FOOT 5 5/8 INCHES	300 GALLON	I FOOT 6 1/8 INCHES
		INFLIGHT FUELING STORE	I FOOT 3 1/8 INCHES

64.) Fuel Cell Probe
65.) Fuel Cell Filler
66.) Fuel Cell
67.) Hoist Receptacle
68.) Engine Support
69.) Slat Track Roller
70.) Wing Fuel Filler
71.) Wink Fuel Tank
72.) Aileron Bellcrank
73.) Slat Track Roller
74.) Aileron Control
75.) Wing Tip
76.) Aileron Tip
77.) Wing Tank Transfer Pump
78.) Elevator Tip

79.) Elevator Tip
80.) Wing Tank Pressure Filler
81.) Unassigned
82.) Aileron Tip
83.) Wing Tip
84.) Aileron Control
85.) Slat Track Rollers
86.) Aileron Bellcrank
87.) Slat Track Roller
88.) Fuel Quantity Probe
89.) Fuel Quantity Probe

90.) Oil Tank Filler
91.) Wing Tank Vent Lines
92.) Identification Antenna (IFF)
93.) Elapsed Time Clock Transformer
94.) Engine Compartment
95.) Unassigned
96.) Unassigned
97.) Unassigned
98.) Unassigned

99.) AN/APG-53A Radar
100.) AN/ARA-25 Antenna
100A.) ECM Preamplifier AFC 325
101.) Door Latch Inspection
102.) Nose Gear Door Forward
103.) Nose Gear Aft Door
104.) Actuating Cylinder Attaching Bolt
105.) Hydraulic Fluid Cooler/Fuel Filter
106.) Fuel Cell Drain
107.) Engine Compartment
108.) External Power Receptacle
109.) Approach Light
110.) Main Gear Forward Door
111.) Main Gear Aft Door
112.) Wing Slat Track
113.) Tiedown Ring
114.) Wing Slat Center Track
115.) Wing Slat Outboard Slat
116.) Slat Track Stop
117.) Trim Tab Jackscrew
118.) Aileron Flutter Damper
119.) Flutter Damper Inspection
120.) External Stores Rack
121.) Aft Gear Door Actuating Cylinder
122.) External Stores Rack

131.) Slat Track Stop
132.) Slat Outboard Track
133.) Slat Center Track
134.) Tiedown Ring
135.) Slat Inboard Track
136.) Main Gear Aft Door
137.) Main Gear Forward Door
138.) Engine Door
138A.) Starter Probe Door
139.) Nose Gear Actuating
      Cylinder Attaching Bolt
140.) Emergency Generator Upper
      Door
141.) Emergency Generator Lowe
      Door
142.) Electronic Countermeasures
      Antenna AFC 325 & 394

123.) Automatic Flight Controls
123A.) Identification Antenna (IFF)
123B.) Aft Chaff Dispenser Cover AFC 325
124.) Liquid Oxygen Compartment
124A.) Forward Chaff Dispenser Cover AFC 325
125.) Engine Compartment
126.) Wing Tank Fuel Drain
127.) Aft Gear Door Actuating Cylinder
128.) External Stores Rack
129.) Flutter Damper Inspection
130.) Aileron Flutter Damper

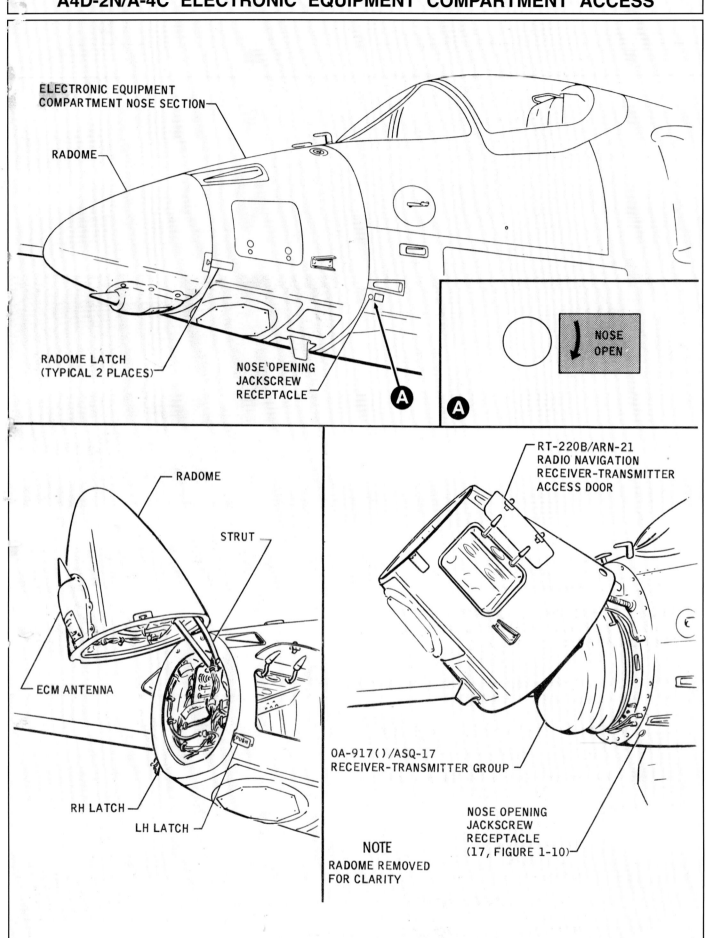

ELECTRONIC EQUIPMENT
COMPARTMENT NOSE SECTION

RADOME

RADOME LATCH
(TYPICAL 2 PLACES)

NOSE OPENING
JACKSCREW
RECEPTACLE

A

A

NOSE
OPEN

RADOME

STRUT

ECM ANTENNA

RH LATCH

LH LATCH

NOTE
RADOME REMOVED
FOR CLARITY

RT-220B/ARN-21
RADIO NAVIGATION
RECEIVER-TRANSMITTER
ACCESS DOOR

OA-917()/ASQ-17
RECEIVER-TRANSMITTER GROUP

NOSE OPENING
JACKSCREW
RECEPTACLE
(17, FIGURE 1-10)

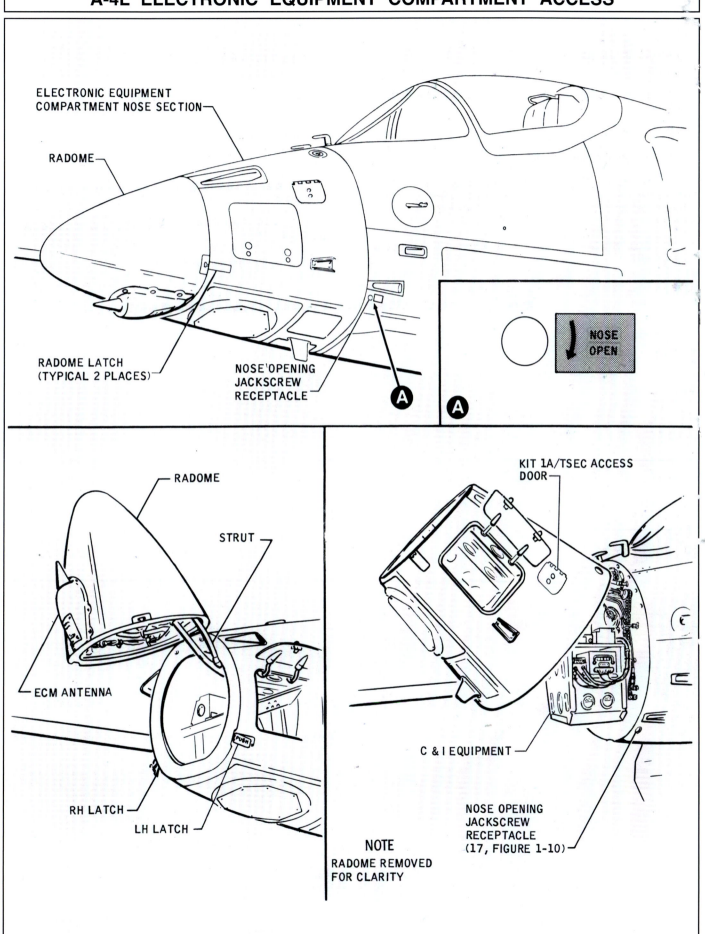

ELECTRONIC EQUIPMENT
COMPARTMENT NOSE SECTION

RADOME

RADOME LATCH
(TYPICAL 2 PLACES)

NOSE OPENING
JACKSCREW
RECEPTACLE

Ⓐ

Ⓐ

NOSE
OPEN

RADOME

STRUT

ECM ANTENNA

RH LATCH

LH LATCH

PUSH

KIT 1A/TSEC ACCESS
DOOR

C & I EQUIPMENT

NOSE OPENING
JACKSCREW
RECEPTACLE
(17, FIGURE 1-10)

NOTE
RADOME REMOVED
FOR CLARITY

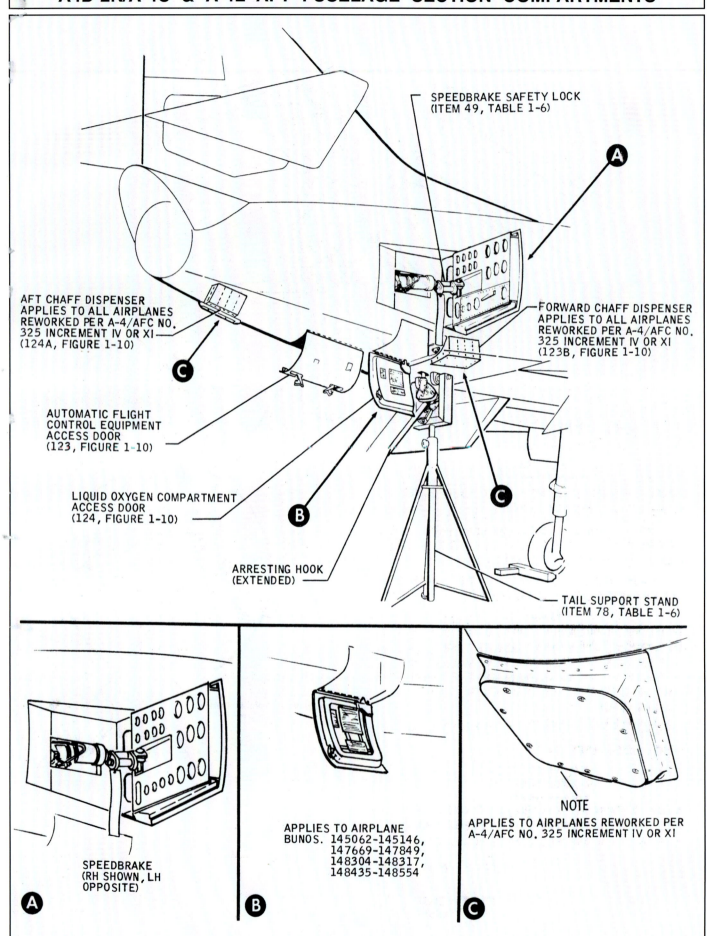

SPEEDBRAKE SAFETY LOCK
(ITEM 49, TABLE 1-6)

Ⓐ

AFT CHAFF DISPENSER
APPLIES TO ALL AIRPLANES
REWORKED PER A-4/AFC NO.
325 INCREMENT IV OR XI
(124A, FIGURE 1-10)

Ⓒ

FORWARD CHAFF DISPENSER
APPLIES TO ALL AIRPLANES
REWORKED PER A-4/AFC NO.
325 INCREMENT IV OR XI
(123B, FIGURE 1-10)

AUTOMATIC FLIGHT
CONTROL EQUIPMENT
ACCESS DOOR
(123, FIGURE 1-10)

LIQUID OXYGEN COMPARTMENT
ACCESS DOOR
(124, FIGURE 1-10)

Ⓒ

Ⓑ

ARRESTING HOOK
(EXTENDED)

TAIL SUPPORT STAND
(ITEM 78, TABLE 1-6)

SPEEDBRAKE
(RH SHOWN, LH
OPPOSITE)

Ⓐ

APPLIES TO AIRPLANE
BUNOS. 145062-145146,
147669-147849,
148304-148317,
148435-148554

Ⓑ

NOTE
APPLIES TO AIRPLANES REWORKED PER
A-4/AFC NO. 325 INCREMENT IV OR XI

Ⓒ

A-4L ECM/ELECTRONICS HUMP ACCESS AND INSPECTION PROVISIONS

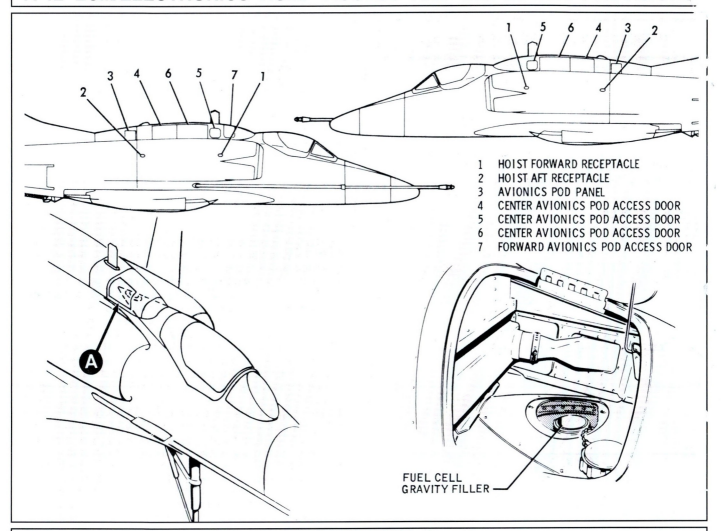

1 HOIST FORWARD RECEPTACLE
2 HOIST AFT RECEPTACLE
3 AVIONICS POD PANEL
4 CENTER AVIONICS POD ACCESS DOOR
5 CENTER AVIONICS POD ACCESS DOOR
6 CENTER AVIONICS POD ACCESS DOOR
7 FORWARD AVIONICS POD ACCESS DOOR

FUEL CELL
GRAVITY FILLER

A-4L SPOILERS

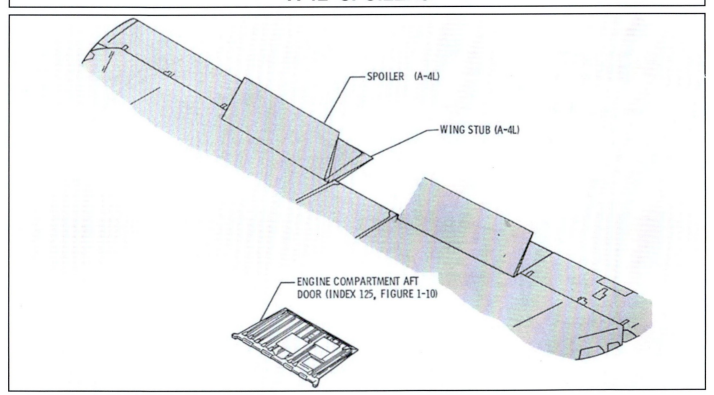

SPOILER (A-4L)

WING STUB (A-4L)

ENGINE COMPARTMENT AFT
DOOR (INDEX 125, FIGURE 1-10)

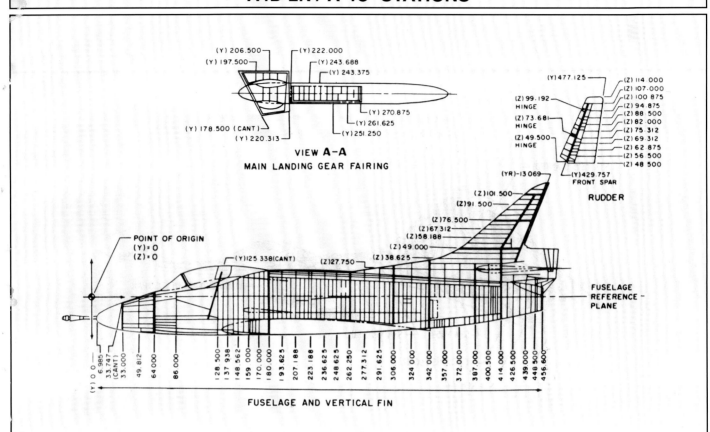

VIEW **A-A**

MAIN LANDING GEAR FAIRING

RUDDER

FUSELAGE AND VERTICAL FIN

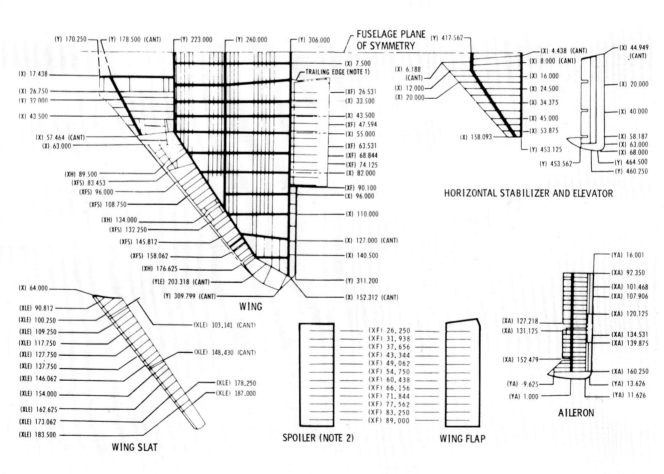

FUSELAGE PLANE OF SYMMETRY

HORIZONTAL STABILIZER AND ELEVATOR

WING

WING SLAT

SPOILER (NOTE 2)

WING FLAP

AILERON

SEC Y-Y
FUS STA 400.500
DWG NO 9667149

SEC W-W
FUS STA 382.000
DWG NO 9667148

SEC V-V
FUS STA 372.000
DWG NO 9667147

SEC U-U
FUS STA 357.000
DWG NO 9667146

SEC J-J
FUS STA 414.000
DWG NO 9545175

SEC H-H
FUS STA 342.000
DWG NO 9545170

SEC G-G
FUS STA 262.000
DWG NO 9545165

SEC F-F
FUS STA 223.188
DWG NO 9442762

SEC E-E
FUS STA 180.000
DWG NO 9442760

SEC K-K
VERTICAL STABILIZER
Z - 76.500
DWG NO 9442732

SEC D-D
FUS STA 125.338 CANT
DWG NO 9442752

SEC C-C
FUS STA 86.000
DWG NO 9667113

SEC B-B
FUS STA 64.000
DWG NO 9667112

SEC A-A
FUS STA 33.250
DWG NO 5660826

STATIC GROUND LINE

17

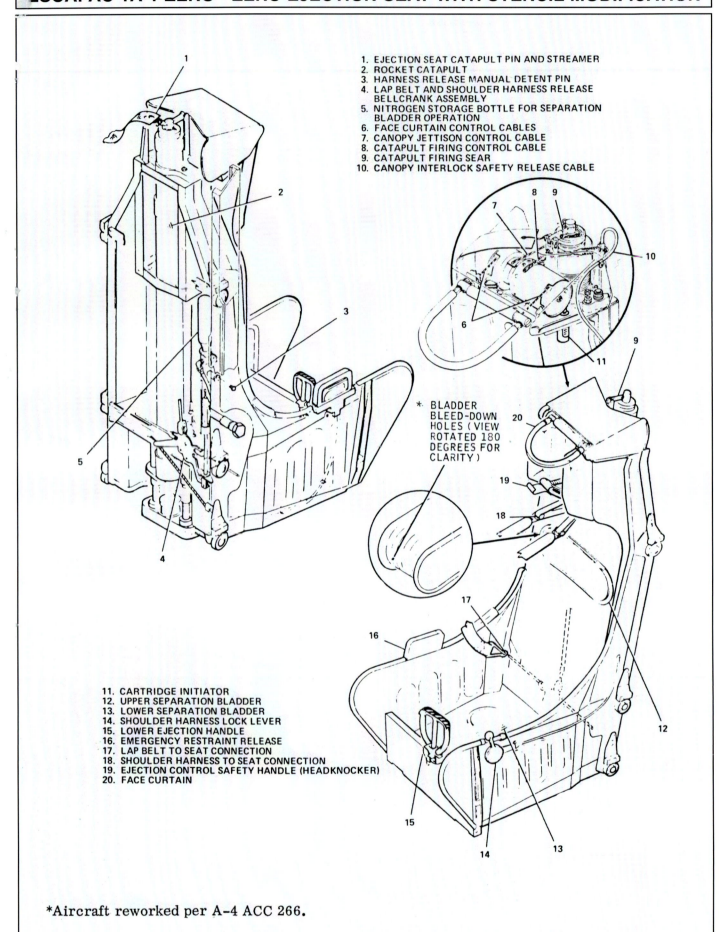

1. EJECTION SEAT CATAPULT PIN AND STREAMER
2. ROCKET CATAPULT
3. HARNESS RELEASE MANUAL DETENT PIN
4. LAP BELT AND SHOULDER HARNESS RELEASE BELLCRANK ASSEMBLY
5. NITROGEN STORAGE BOTTLE FOR SEPARATION BLADDER OPERATION
6. FACE CURTAIN CONTROL CABLES
7. CANOPY JETTISON CONTROL CABLE
8. CATAPULT FIRING CONTROL CABLE
9. CATAPULT FIRING SEAR
10. CANOPY INTERLOCK SAFETY RELEASE CABLE

*. BLADDER BLEED-DOWN HOLES (VIEW ROTATED 180 DEGREES FOR CLARITY)

11. CARTRIDGE INITIATOR
12. UPPER SEPARATION BLADDER
13. LOWER SEPARATION BLADDER
14. SHOULDER HARNESS LOCK LEVER
15. LOWER EJECTION HANDLE
16. EMERGENCY RESTRAINT RELEASE
17. LAP BELT TO SEAT CONNECTION
18. SHOULDER HARNESS TO SEAT CONNECTION
19. EJECTION CONTROL SAFETY HANDLE (HEADKNOCKER)
20. FACE CURTAIN

*Aircraft reworked per A-4 ACC 266.

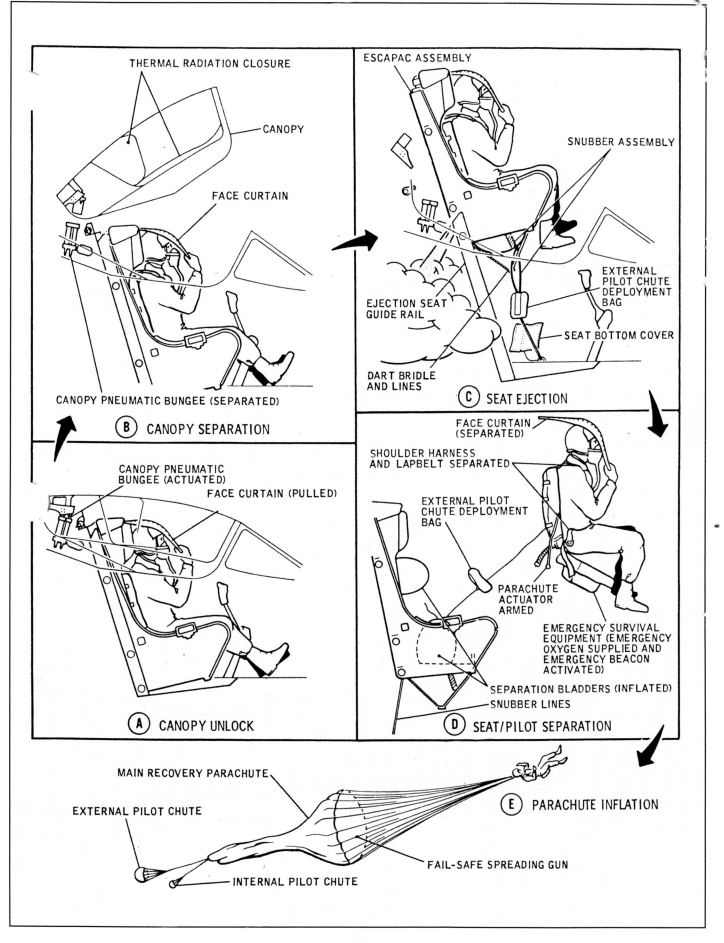

THERMAL RADIATION CLOSURE

CANOPY

FACE CURTAIN

CANOPY PNEUMATIC BUNGEE (SEPARATED)

B CANOPY SEPARATION

ESCAPAC ASSEMBLY

SNUBBER ASSEMBLY

EJECTION SEAT GUIDE RAIL

EXTERNAL PILOT CHUTE DEPLOYMENT BAG

SEAT BOTTOM COVER

DART BRIDLE AND LINES

C SEAT EJECTION

CANOPY PNEUMATIC BUNGEE (ACTUATED)

FACE CURTAIN (PULLED)

A CANOPY UNLOCK

FACE CURTAIN (SEPARATED)

SHOULDER HARNESS AND LAPBELT SEPARATED

EXTERNAL PILOT CHUTE DEPLOYMENT BAG

PARACHUTE ACTUATOR ARMED

EMERGENCY SURVIVAL EQUIPMENT (EMERGENCY OXYGEN SUPPLIED AND EMERGENCY BEACON ACTIVATED)

SEPARATION BLADDERS (INFLATED)

SNUBBER LINES

D SEAT/PILOT SEPARATION

MAIN RECOVERY PARACHUTE

EXTERNAL PILOT CHUTE

INTERNAL PILOT CHUTE

FAIL-SAFE SPREADING GUN

E PARACHUTE INFLATION

A4D-2N / A-4C INSTRUMENT PANEL

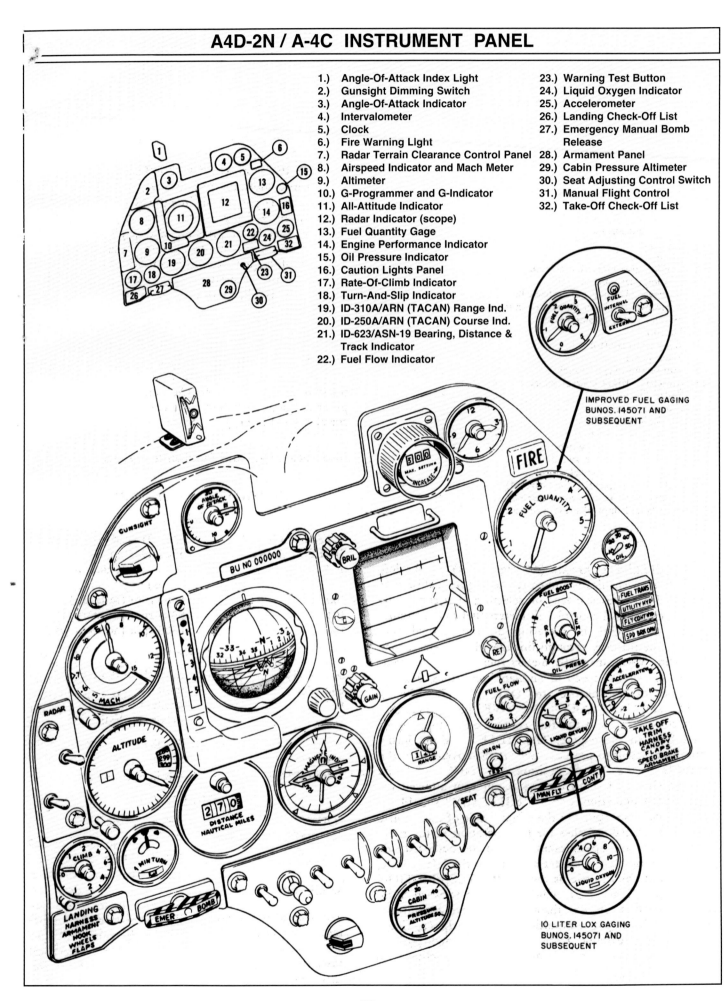

1.) Angle-Of-Attack Index Light
2.) Gunsight Dimming Switch
3.) Angle-Of-Attack Indicator
4.) Intervalometer
5.) Clock
6.) Fire Warning Light
7.) Radar Terrain Clearance Control Panel
8.) Airspeed Indicator and Mach Meter
9.) Altimeter
10.) G-Programmer and G-Indicator
11.) All-Attitude Indicator
12.) Radar Indicator (scope)
13.) Fuel Quantity Gage
14.) Engine Performance Indicator
15.) Oil Pressure Indicator
16.) Caution Lights Panel
17.) Rate-Of-Climb Indicator
18.) Turn-And-Slip Indicator
19.) ID-310A/ARN (TACAN) Range Ind.
20.) ID-250A/ARN (TACAN) Course Ind.
21.) ID-623/ASN-19 Bearing, Distance & Track Indicator
22.) Fuel Flow Indicator

23.) Warning Test Button
24.) Liquid Oxygen Indicator
25.) Accelerometer
26.) Landing Check-Off List
27.) Emergency Manual Bomb Release
28.) Armament Panel
29.) Cabin Pressure Altimeter
30.) Seat Adjusting Control Switch
31.) Manual Flight Control
32.) Take-Off Check-Off List

IMPROVED FUEL GAGING
BUNOS. 145071 AND
SUBSEQUENT

IO LITER LOX GAGING
BUNOS. 145071 AND
SUBSEQUENT

KEY

1. GUNSIGHT DIMMING SWITCH
2. GUNSIGHT ELEVATION CONTROL
3. SKID INDICATOR
4. GUNSIGHT REFLECTOR PLATE
5. REFLECTOR PLATE STABILIZING STRUT
6. GUNSIGHT
7. LOCKING YOKE HANDLE
8. ELEVATION CONTROL GUARD

9. EMERGENCY BOMB MANUAL RELEASE HANDLE
10. EMERGENCY STATIONS SELECT SWITCH
11. MASTER ARMAMENT SWITCH
12. FUNCTION SELECTOR SWITCH
13. ARMAMENT PANEL (EXCEPT CABIN ALTIMETER AND SEAT SWITCH)
14. GUNS SWITCH
15. BOMB ARMING SWITCH
16. STATIONS SELECTOR SWITCHES

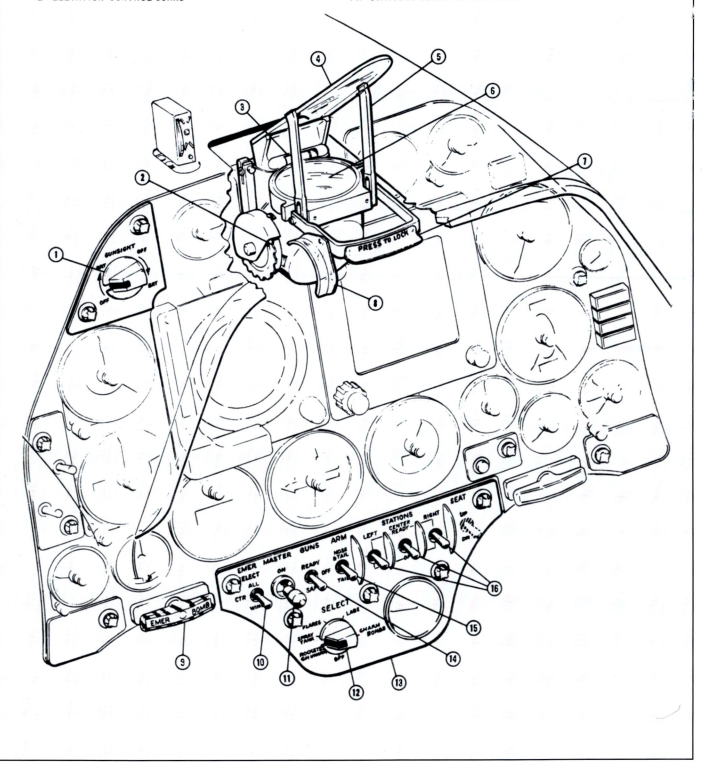

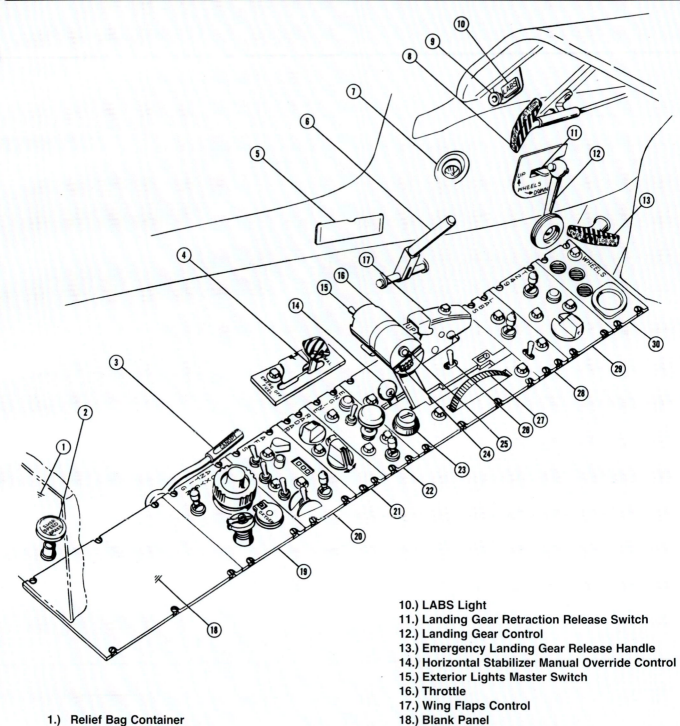

10.) LABS Light
11.) Landing Gear Retraction Release Switch
12.) Landing Gear Control
13.) Emergency Landing Gear Release Handle
14.) Horizontal Stabilizer Manual Override Control
15.) Exterior Lights Master Switch
16.) Throttle
17.) Wing Flaps Control
18.) Blank Panel
19.) Anti-G and Oxygen Panel
20.) Automatic Flight Control Panel
21.) Radar Control Panel
22.) Engine Control Panel
23.) Rudder Trim Switch
24.) Speedbrakes Switch
25.) Radio Microphone Switch
26.) Air Starting Ignition Switch
27.) Throttle Friction Wheel
28.) LABS Control Panel (when carried)
29.) T-249 Control Panel (when carried)
30.) Wheels and Flaps Position Indicators

1.) Relief Bag Container
2.) Emergency Speedbrake Control
3.) Canopy Control (manual)
4.) Manual Fuel Shut-Off Control
5.) Airspeed Calibration Card
6.) Catapult Handgrip
7.) Air Conditioning Eyeball Diffuser
8.) Canopy Jettison Handle
9.) TO Light

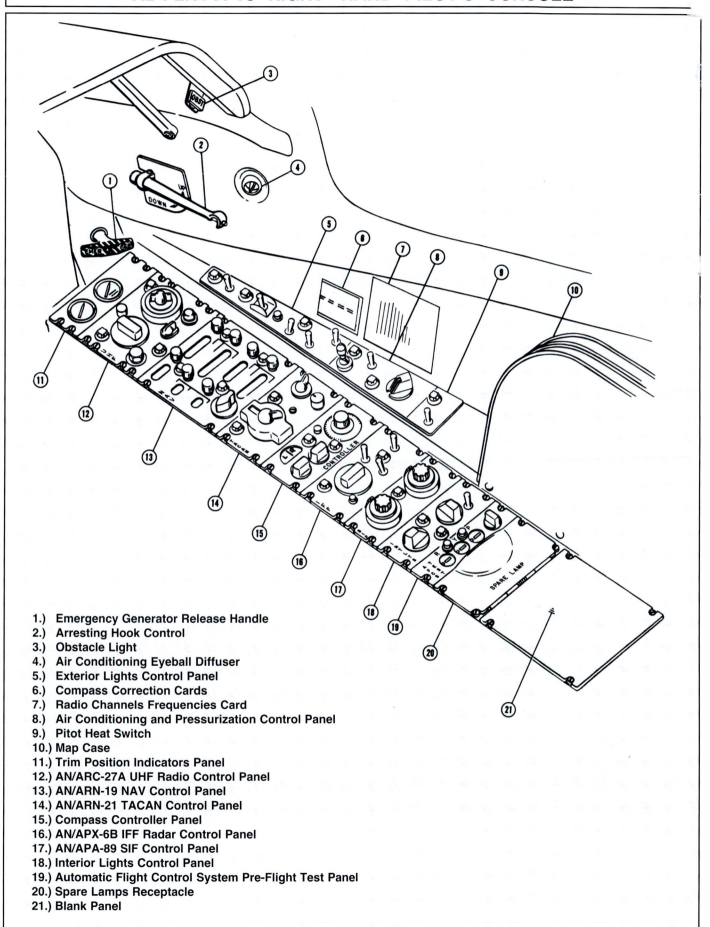

1.) Emergency Generator Release Handle
2.) Arresting Hook Control
3.) Obstacle Light
4.) Air Conditioning Eyeball Diffuser
5.) Exterior Lights Control Panel
6.) Compass Correction Cards
7.) Radio Channels Frequencies Card
8.) Air Conditioning and Pressurization Control Panel
9.) Pitot Heat Switch
10.) Map Case
11.) Trim Position Indicators Panel
12.) AN/ARC-27A UHF Radio Control Panel
13.) AN/ARN-19 NAV Control Panel
14.) AN/ARN-21 TACAN Control Panel
15.) Compass Controller Panel
16.) AN/APX-6B IFF Radar Control Panel
17.) AN/APA-89 SIF Control Panel
18.) Interior Lights Control Panel
19.) Automatic Flight Control System Pre-Flight Test Panel
20.) Spare Lamps Receptacle
21.) Blank Panel

AD4-2N / A-4C / A-4L COCKPIT GENERAL ARRANGEMENT

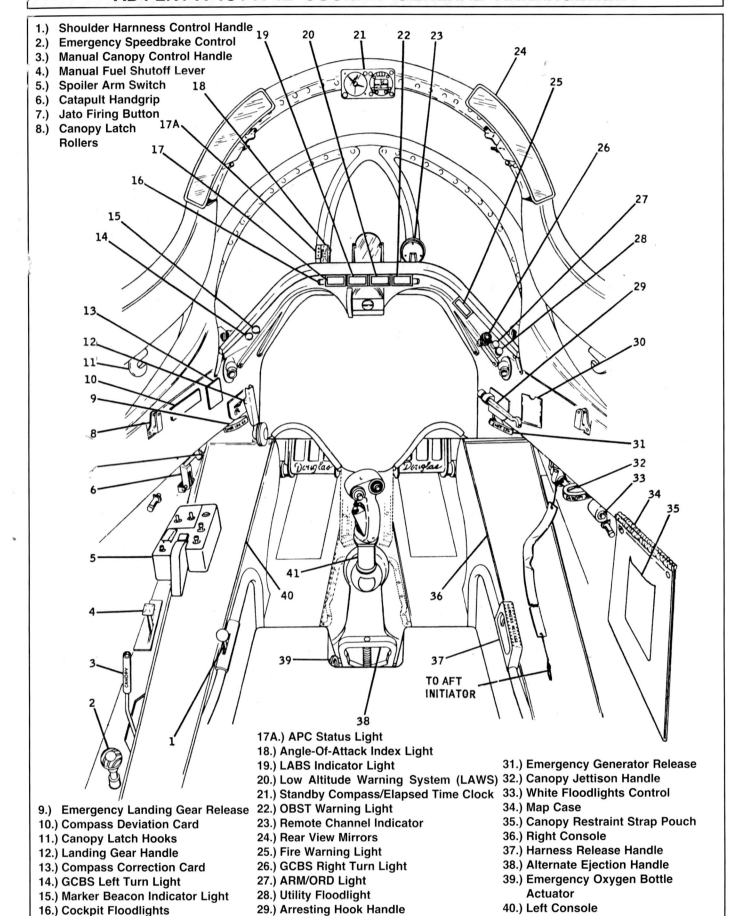

1.) Shoulder Harness Control Handle
2.) Emergency Speedbrake Control
3.) Manual Canopy Control Handle
4.) Manual Fuel Shutoff Lever
5.) Spoiler Arm Switch
6.) Catapult Handgrip
7.) Jato Firing Button
8.) Canopy Latch Rollers

9.) Emergency Landing Gear Release
10.) Compass Deviation Card
11.) Canopy Latch Hooks
12.) Landing Gear Handle
13.) Compass Correction Card
14.) GCBS Left Turn Light
15.) Marker Beacon Indicator Light
16.) Cockpit Floodlights
17.) Wheels Warning Light

17A.) APC Status Light
18.) Angle-Of-Attack Index Light
19.) LABS Indicator Light
20.) Low Altitude Warning System (LAWS)
21.) Standby Compass/Elapsed Time Clock
22.) OBST Warning Light
23.) Remote Channel Indicator
24.) Rear View Mirrors
25.) Fire Warning Light
26.) GCBS Right Turn Light
27.) ARM/ORD Light
28.) Utility Floodlight
29.) Arresting Hook Handle
30.) Standby Compass Deviation Card

31.) Emergency Generator Release
32.) Canopy Jettison Handle
33.) White Floodlights Control
34.) Map Case
35.) Canopy Restraint Strap Pouch
36.) Right Console
37.) Harness Release Handle
38.) Alternate Ejection Handle
39.) Emergency Oxygen Bottle Actuator
40.) Left Console
41.) Control Stick

TO AFT INITIATOR

SEARCH

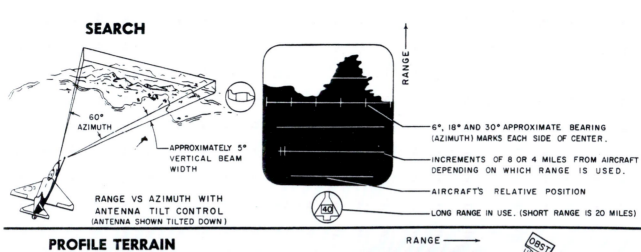

60° AZIMUTH

APPROXIMATELY 5° VERTICAL BEAM WIDTH

RANGE VS AZIMUTH WITH ANTENNA TILT CONTROL (ANTENNA SHOWN TILTED DOWN)

6°, 18° AND 30° APPROXIMATE BEARING (AZIMUTH) MARKS EACH SIDE OF CENTER.

INCREMENTS OF 8 OR 4 MILES FROM AIRCRAFT DEPENDING ON WHICH RANGE IS USED.

AIRCRAFT'S RELATIVE POSITION

LONG RANGE IN USE. (SHORT RANGE IS 20 MILES)

PROFILE TERRAIN CLEARANCE

RANGE VS ANTENNA DEPRESSION ANGLE (10° ABOVE AND 15° BELOW FLIGHT PATH)

NOTE
ANTENNA TILT CONTROL IS INEFFECTIVE AND NOT USED IN THIS MODE.

AIRCRAFT'S RELATIVE POSITION ON FLIGHT PATH

SHORT RANGE IN USE. (LONG RANGE IS 20 MILES)

INCREMENTS OF 2 OR 4 MILES (DEPENDING ON WHICH RANGE IS USED) ALONG FLIGHT PATH LINE

IMAGINARY LEVEL 1000 FEET BELOW AIRCRAFT'S FLIGHT PATH. (DISTORTION BUILT INTO SCOPE)

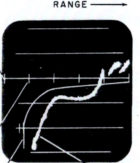

RANGE

PILOT WARNINGS (OBSTACLE LIGHT AND AURAL TONE) IF OBSTACLES PROTRUDE ABOVE IMAGINARY LEVEL 1000 FEET BELOW AIRCRAFT'S FLIGHT PATH.

VIDEO TRACE INDICATES OBSTACLES IN RELATION TO AIRCRAFT ON FLIGHT PATH AND TO 1000 FOOT LINE.

PLAN TERRAIN CLEARANCE

RANGE VS AZIMUTH ON AIRCRAFT'S FLIGHT PATH (ALSO ANTENNA TILT CONTROL)

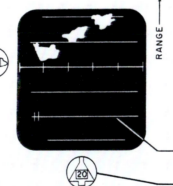

PLAN AND SEARCH MODES ARE IDENTICAL EXCEPT:
(A) PLAN IS NORMALLY USED AT AIRCRAFT'S FLIGHT PATH LINE;
(B) SEARCH HAS LONGER RANGES (40 AND 20) THAN PLAN (20 AND 10);
(C) IN PLAN, DETAIL CONTROL REFINES VERTICAL BEAM WIDTH DOWN TO 1 DEGREE. DETAIL IS INEFFECTIVE IN SEARCH MODE;
(D) PROVISIONS ONLY FOR PILOT'S OBSTACLE WARNINGS ARE AVAILABLE IN PLAN.

INCREMENTS OF 4 OR 2 MILES FROM AIRCRAFT DEPENDING ON WHICH RANGE IS USED.

LONG RANGE IN USE. (SHORT RANGE IS 10 MILES)

AIR-TO-GROUND RANGING

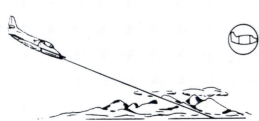

SLANT RANGE TO SURFACE ALONG BORESIGHT LINE WITH ZERO AZIMUTH

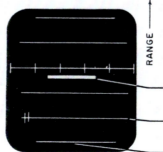

ANTENNA TILT CONTROL IS INEFFECTIVE AND SHOULD NOT BE USED IN THIS MODE.

THIS MODE REQUIRES A 10° DIVE OR GREATER TO LOCK-ON THE SURFACE WITHIN 15,000 YARDS.

BAR INDICATES SURFACE DISTANCE FROM AIRCRAFT

4000 YARD INCREMENTS FROM AIRCRAFT. (TOTAL MAXIMUM RANGE = 15,000 YARDS (7 1/2 NAUTICAL MILES))

AIRCRAFT'S RELATIVE POSITION

NOTE
NO RANGE BOXES ARE USED IN THIS MODE.

UPGRADED A-4C / A-4L INSTRUMENT PANELS

1.) Wheels and Flaps Panel
2.) Friction Lock Control
3.) Radio Microphone Switch
4.) Speedbrake Switch
5.) Engine Control Panel
6.) Radar Control Panel
7.) AFCS Panel
8.) Life Systems Control Panel
9.) Emergency Speedbrake
Control
11.) Beacon Radar Control
12.) Manual Fuel Shutoff Control
Lever

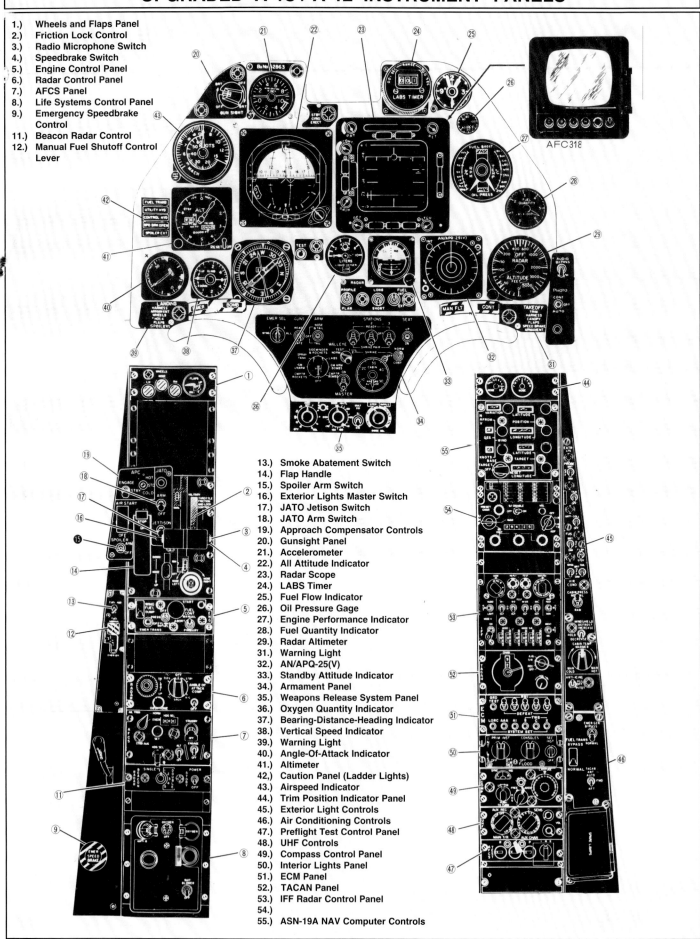

AFC318

13.) Smoke Abatement Switch
14.) Flap Handle
15.) Spoiler Arm Switch
16.) Exterior Lights Master Switch
17.) JATO Jetison Switch
18.) JATO Arm Switch
19.) Approach Compensator Controls
20.) Gunsight Panel
21.) Accelerometer
22.) All Attitude Indicator
23.) Radar Scope
24.) LABS Timer
25.) Fuel Flow Indicator
26.) Oil Pressure Gage
27.) Engine Performance Indicator
28.) Fuel Quantity Indicator
29.) Radar Altimeter
31.) Warning Light
32.) AN/APQ-25(V)
33.) Standby Attitude Indicator
34.) Armament Panel
35.) Weapons Release System Panel
36.) Oxygen Quantity Indicator
37.) Bearing-Distance-Heading Indicator
38.) Vertical Speed Indicator
39.) Warning Light
40.) Angle-Of-Attack Indicator
41.) Altimeter
42,) Caution Panel (Ladder Lights)
43.) Airspeed Indicator
44.) Trim Position Indicator Panel
45.) Exterior Light Controls
46.) Air Conditioning Controls
47.) Preflight Test Control Panel
48.) UHF Controls
49.) Compass Control Panel
50.) Interior Lights Panel
51.) ECM Panel
52.) TACAN Panel
53.) IFF Radar Control Panel
54.)
55.) ASN-19A NAV Computer Controls

A-4L INSTRUMENT PANEL

The limited all-weather capability added to the A4D-2N/A-4C by the inclusion of the Westinghouse APG-53A terrain-clearance radar required a major re-alignment of the cockpit. The principal problem was to find room for the 5-inch square AJB-3 radar display. Other changes were that the armament panel was moved downward and the instruments and controls were rearranged on the instrument panel.

The APG-53A operated in four modes. It had basic search, air-to-ground ranging, and two terrain-clearance modes. These were plan and profile. Its tactical range was forty miles with an elevation of +10° up and -15° down off level flight. Like the Skyhawk it was extremely lightweight at only 90 pounds.

20MM GUNNERY EQUIPMENT

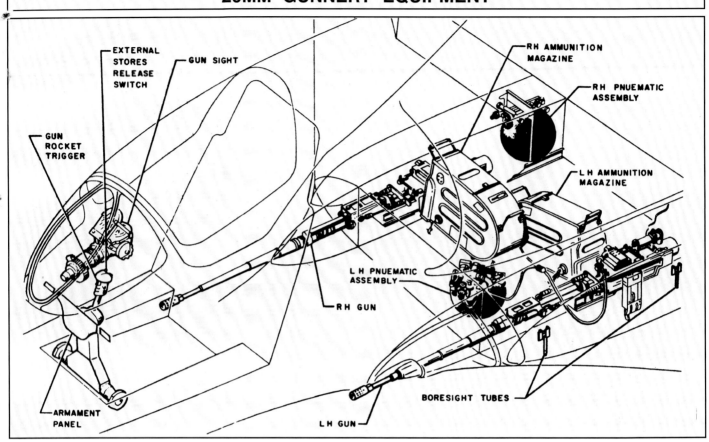

EXTERNAL STORES RELEASE SWITCH

GUN SIGHT

RH AMMUNITION MAGAZINE

RH PNUEMATIC ASSEMBLY

GUN ROCKET TRIGGER

L H AMMUNITION MAGAZINE

L H PNUEMATIC ASSEMBLY

RH GUN

BORESIGHT TUBES

ARMAMENT PANEL

L H GUN

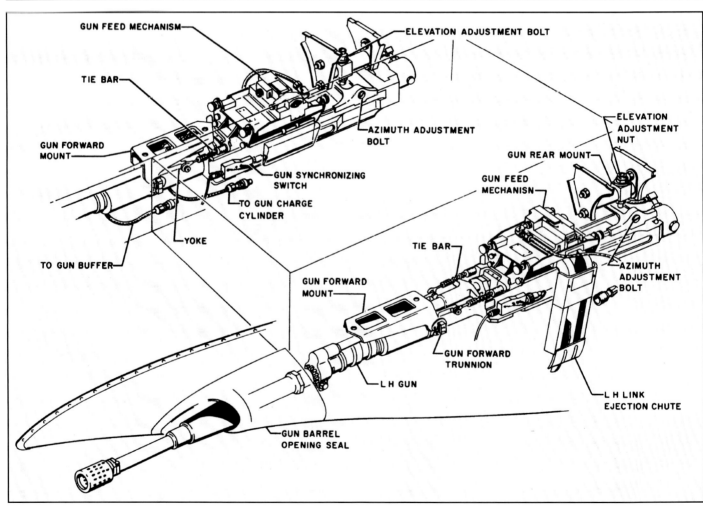

GUN FEED MECHANISM

ELEVATION ADJUSTMENT BOLT

TIE BAR

ELEVATION ADJUSTMENT NUT

GUN FORWARD MOUNT

GUN REAR MOUNT

GUN FEED MECHANISN

AZIMUTH ADJUSTMENT BOLT

GUN SYNCHRONIZING SWITCH

TO GUN CHARGE CYLINDER

TIE BAR

YOKE

AZIMUTH ADJUSTMENT BOLT

TO GUN BUFFER

GUN FORWARD MOUNT

GUN FORWARD TRUNNION

L H LINK EJECTION CHUTE

L H GUN

GUN BARREL OPENING SEAL

GUN REMOVAL AND INSTALLATION

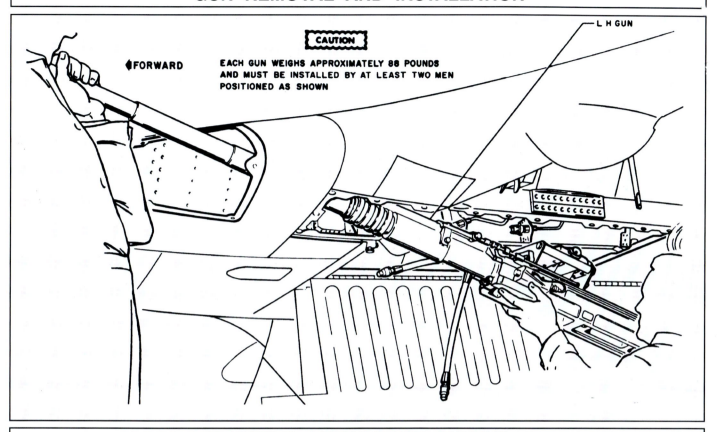

◄FORWARD

CAUTION

EACH GUN WEIGHS APPROXIMATELY 88 POUNDS AND MUST BE INSTALLED BY AT LEAST TWO MEN POSITIONED AS SHOWN

L H GUN

FLEXIBLE AMMUNITION CHUTES

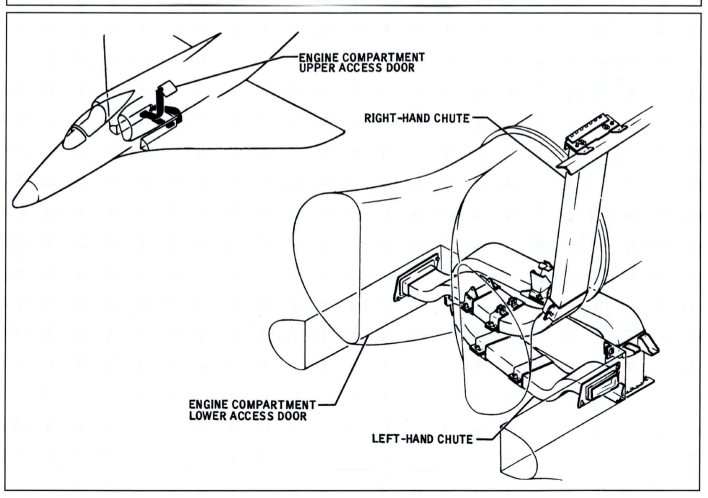

ENGINE COMPARTMENT UPPER ACCESS DOOR

RIGHT-HAND CHUTE

ENGINE COMPARTMENT LOWER ACCESS DOOR

LEFT-HAND CHUTE

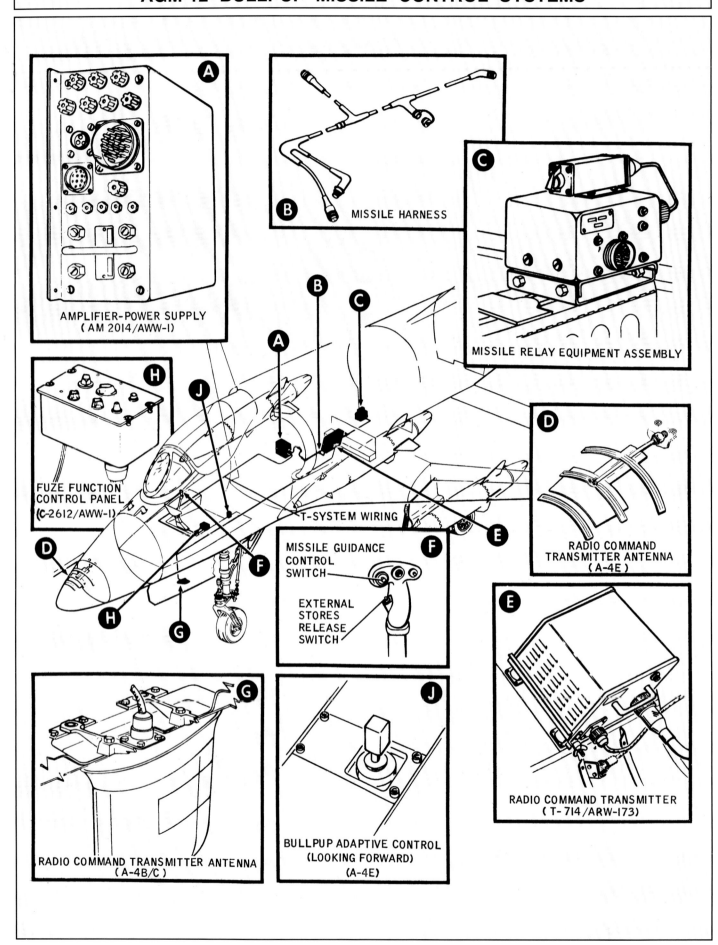

A

AMPLIFIER-POWER SUPPLY
(AM 2014/AWW-I)

B MISSILE HARNESS

C MISSILE RELAY EQUIPMENT ASSEMBLY

H FUZE FUNCTION CONTROL PANEL
(C-2612/AWW-1)

T-SYSTEM WIRING

D RADIO COMMAND TRANSMITTER ANTENNA
(A-4E)

F MISSILE GUIDANCE CONTROL SWITCH

EXTERNAL STORES RELEASE SWITCH

E RADIO COMMAND TRANSMITTER
(T-714/ARW-173)

G RADIO COMMAND TRANSMITTER ANTENNA
(A-4B/C)

J BULLPUP ADAPTIVE CONTROL
(LOOKING FORWARD)
(A-4E)

AGM-12 BULLPUP MISSILE CONTROL SYSTEMS

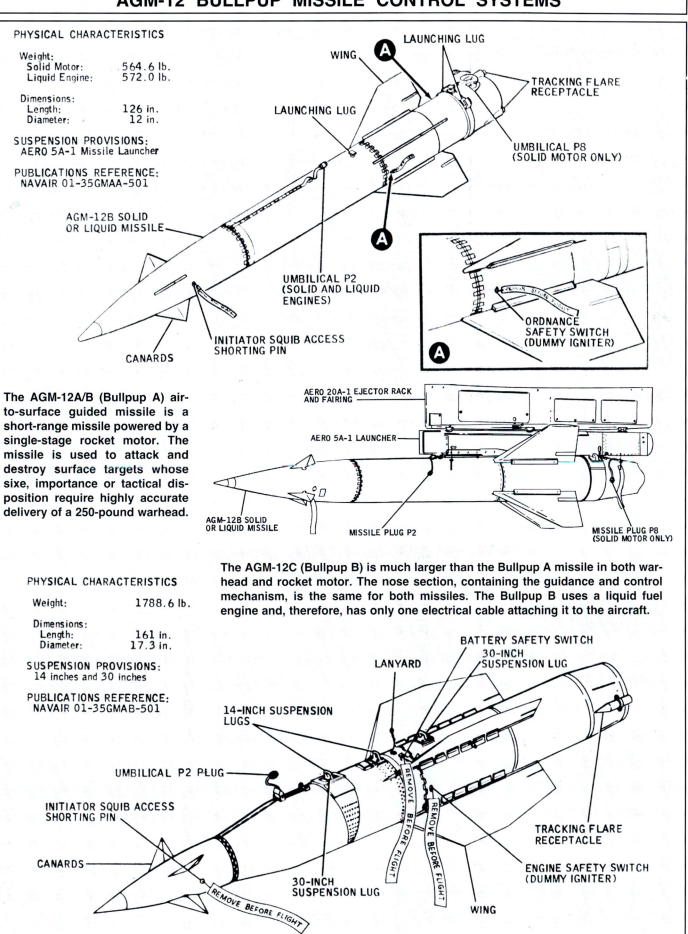

PHYSICAL CHARACTERISTICS

Weight:
Solid Motor: 564.6 lb.
Liquid Engine: 572.0 lb.

Dimensions:
Length: 126 in.
Diameter: 12 in.

SUSPENSION PROVISIONS:
AERO 5A-1 Missile Launcher

PUBLICATIONS REFERENCE:
NAVAIR 01-35GMAA-501

LAUNCHING LUG
WING
A
LAUNCHING LUG
TRACKING FLARE RECEPTACLE
UMBILICAL P8 (SOLID MOTOR ONLY)
A
AGM-12B SOLID OR LIQUID MISSILE
UMBILICAL P2 (SOLID AND LIQUID ENGINES)
INITIATOR SQUIB ACCESS SHORTING PIN
CANARDS
ORDNANCE SAFETY SWITCH (DUMMY IGNITER)
A

The AGM-12A/B (Bullpup A) air-to-surface guided missile is a short-range missile powered by a single-stage rocket motor. The missile is used to attack and destroy surface targets whose sixe, importance or tactical disposition require highly accurate delivery of a 250-pound warhead.

AERO 20A-1 EJECTOR RACK AND FAIRING
AERO 5A-1 LAUNCHER
AGM-12B SOLID OR LIQUID MISSILE
MISSILE PLUG P2
MISSILE PLUG P8 (SOLID MOTOR ONLY)

The AGM-12C (Bullpup B) is much larger than the Bullpup A missile in both warhead and rocket motor. The nose section, containing the guidance and control mechanism, is the same for both missiles. The Bullpup B uses a liquid fuel engine and, therefore, has only one electrical cable attaching it to the aircraft.

PHYSICAL CHARACTERISTICS

Weight: 1788.6 lb.

Dimensions:
Length: 161 in.
Diameter: 17.3 in.

SUSPENSION PROVISIONS:
14 inches and 30 inches

PUBLICATIONS REFERENCE:
NAVAIR 01-35GMAB-501

BATTERY SAFETY SWITCH
30-INCH SUSPENSION LUG
LANYARD
14-INCH SUSPENSION LUGS
UMBILICAL P2 PLUG
INITIATOR SQUIB ACCESS SHORTING PIN
CANARDS
30-INCH SUSPENSION LUG
TRACKING FLARE RECEPTACLE
ENGINE SAFETY SWITCH (DUMMY IGNITER)
WING
REMOVE BEFORE FLIGHT

MAXIMUM BULLPUP LOADOUT

Above, A4D-2N, BuNo 145069, at Edwards AFB in 1961 with three AGM-12C (Bullpup B) missiles under its wings. (Bob Cooper via Craig Kaston) Below, the Mk. 11 twin 20mm gun was designed by Frank F. Marquardt, a China Lake engineer and packaged in a Mk. 4 gun pod built by the Hughes Tool Company. The pod also carried 750 rounds of ammunition. (USN) Next page, the final Mk. 4 gun pod was more steamlined and three could be fitted on a Skyhawk as seen here on a China Lake A-4C. Three pods could carry 2,250 rounds of 20mm. (NNAM)

Mk. 11 TWIN 20MM GUN

CATAPULT EQUIPMENT FOR TYPICAL STEAM CATAPULT HOOKUP

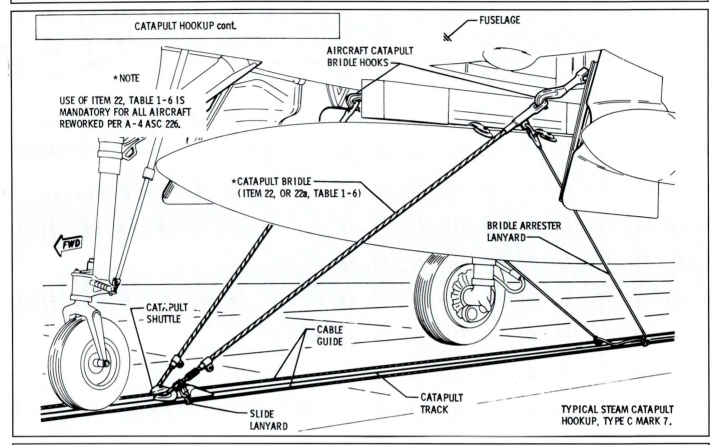

CATAPULT HOOKUP cont.

*NOTE

USE OF ITEM 22, TABLE 1-6 IS MANDATORY FOR ALL AIRCRAFT REWORKED PER A-4 ASC 226.

FWD

FUSELAGE

AIRCRAFT CATAPULT BRIDLE HOOKS

*CATAPULT BRIDLE (ITEM 22, OR 22a, TABLE 1-6)

BRIDLE ARRESTER LANYARD

CATAPULT SHUTTLE

CABLE GUIDE

CATAPULT TRACK

SLIDE LANYARD

TYPICAL STEAM CATAPULT HOOKUP, TYPE C MARK 7.

CATAPULT HOLDBACK FITTING AND TAILHOOK

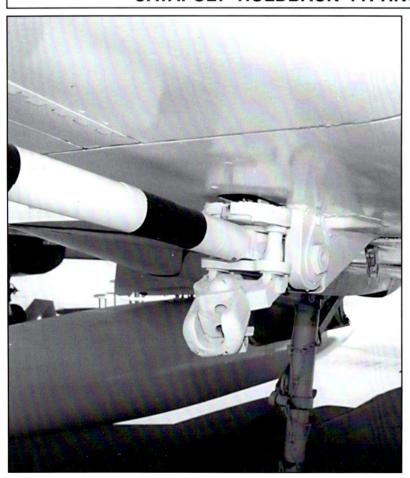

CATAPULT HOOKS AND HOLDBACK FITTING

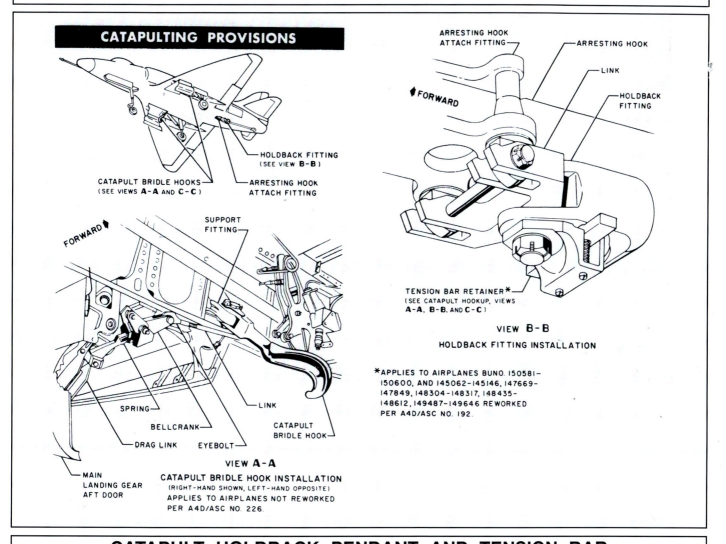

CATAPULTING PROVISIONS

HOLDBACK FITTING
(SEE VIEW **B-B**)

CATAPULT BRIDLE HOOKS
(SEE VIEWS **A-A** AND **C-C**)

ARRESTING HOOK
ATTACH FITTING

ARRESTING HOOK
ATTACH FITTING

ARRESTING HOOK

FORWARD

LINK

HOLDBACK
FITTING

TENSION BAR RETAINER*
(SEE CATAPULT HOOKUP, VIEWS
A-A, **B-B**, AND **C-C**)

VIEW **B-B**

HOLDBACK FITTING INSTALLATION

*APPLIES TO AIRPLANES BUNO. 150581-
150600, AND 145062-145146, 147669-
147849, 148304-148317, 148435-
148612, 149487-149646 REWORKED
PER A4D/ASC NO. 192.

FORWARD

SUPPORT
FITTING

SPRING

BELLCRANK

DRAG LINK

EYEBOLT

LINK

CATAPULT
BRIDLE HOOK

MAIN
LANDING GEAR
AFT DOOR

VIEW **A-A**

CATAPULT BRIDLE HOOK INSTALLATION
(RIGHT-HAND SHOWN, LEFT-HAND OPPOSITE)
APPLIES TO AIRPLANES NOT REWORKED
PER A4D/ASC NO. 226.

CATAPULT HOLDBACK PENDANT AND TENSION BAR

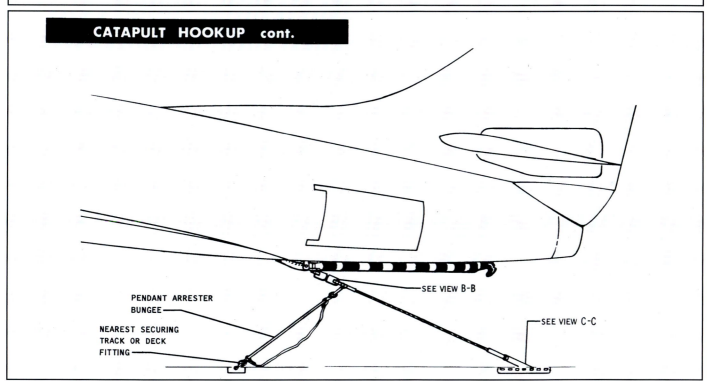

CATAPULT HOOKUP cont.

SEE VIEW B-B

PENDANT ARRESTER
BUNGEE

NEAREST SECURING
TRACK OR DECK
FITTING

SEE VIEW C-C

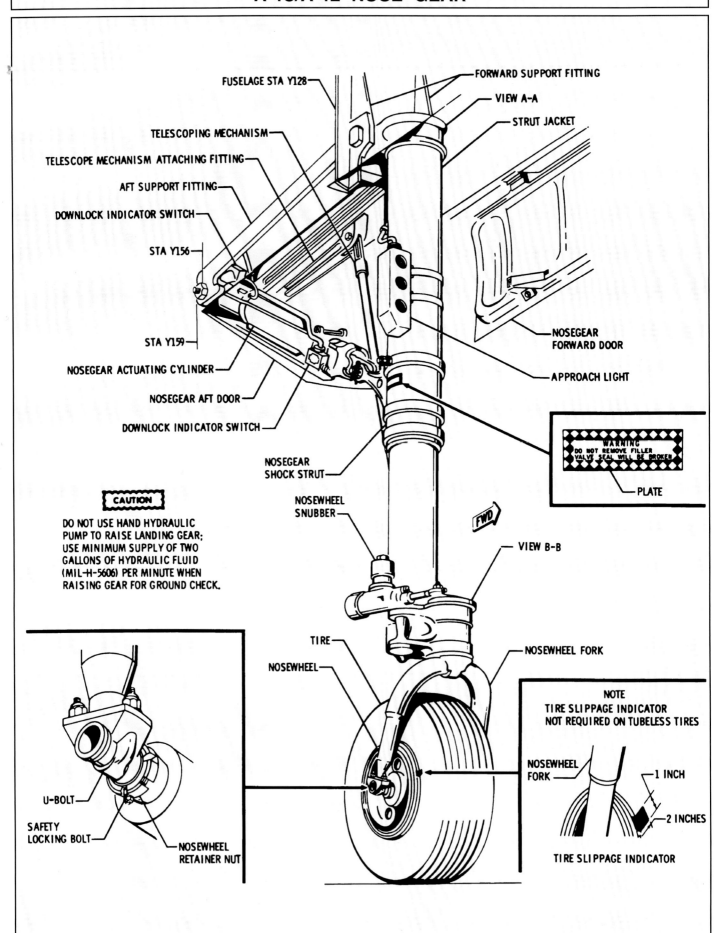

FUSELAGE STA Y128

FORWARD SUPPORT FITTING

VIEW A-A

STRUT JACKET

TELESCOPING MECHANISM

TELESCOPE MECHANISM ATTACHING FITTING

AFT SUPPORT FITTING

DOWNLOCK INDICATOR SWITCH

STA Y156

STA Y159

NOSEGEAR ACTUATING CYLINDER

NOSEGEAR AFT DOOR

DOWNLOCK INDICATOR SWITCH

NOSEGEAR
SHOCK STRUT

NOSEGEAR
FORWARD DOOR

APPROACH LIGHT

WARNING
DO NOT REMOVE FILLER
VALVE SEAL WILL BE BROKEN

PLATE

CAUTION

DO NOT USE HAND HYDRAULIC
PUMP TO RAISE LANDING GEAR;
USE MINIMUM SUPPLY OF TWO
GALLONS OF HYDRAULIC FLUID
(MIL-H-5606) PER MINUTE WHEN
RAISING GEAR FOR GROUND CHECK.

NOSEWHEEL
SNUBBER

FWD

VIEW B-B

TIRE

NOSEWHEEL

NOSEWHEEL FORK

U-BOLT

SAFETY
LOCKING BOLT

NOSEWHEEL
RETAINER NUT

NOTE
TIRE SLIPPAGE INDICATOR
NOT REQUIRED ON TUBELESS TIRES

NOSEWHEEL
FORK

1 INCH

2 INCHES

TIRE SLIPPAGE INDICATOR

Above and below, the aft nose gear door was attached to the nose gear actuating cylinder. At right, the forward nose gear well looking aft. Bottom, forward nose gear door and wheel well. (all Steve Ginter)

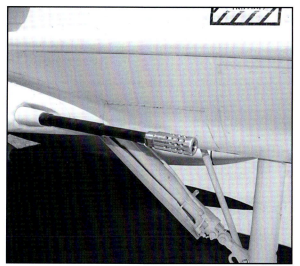

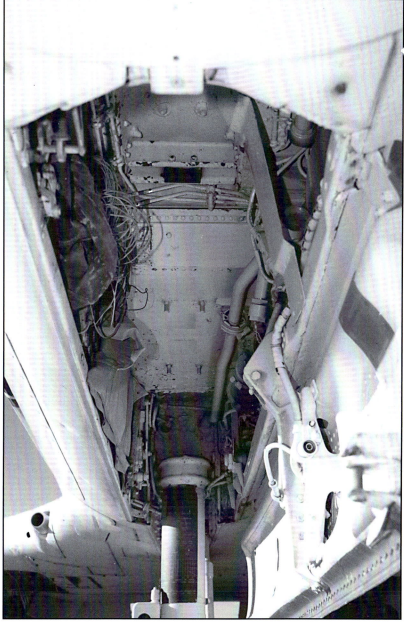

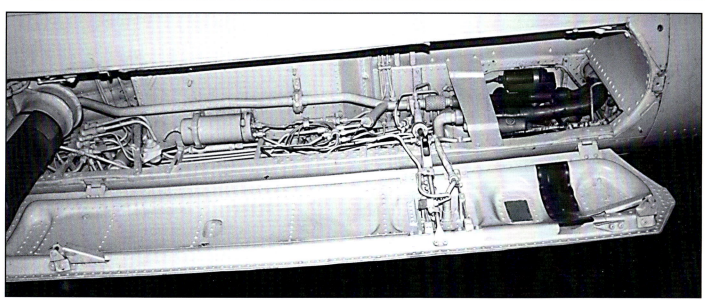

RIGHT - HAND MAIN LANDING GEAR WELL LOOKING AFT

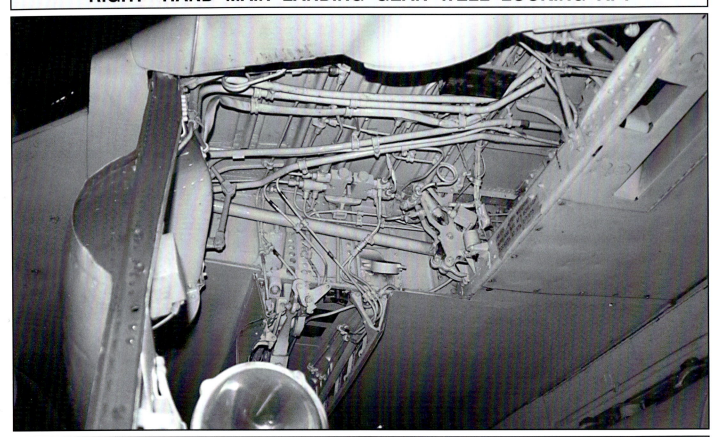

LEFT - HAND MAIN LANDING GEAR WELL LOOKING AFT

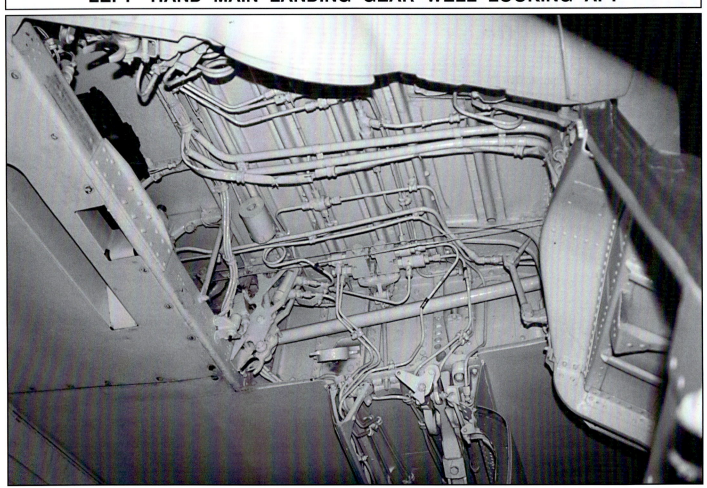

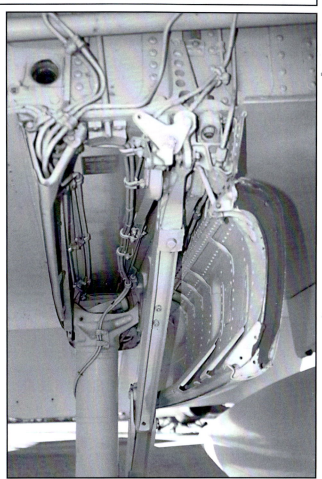

Above, aft left main gear housing and door looking aft and to the right. (Ginter) At right, aft left main gear housing and door looking aft. (Ginter) Bottom, inside of left main gear doors looking outward. The gear, doors and wheel wells were white. The gear doors were painted red around the outer erdges. (Ginter)

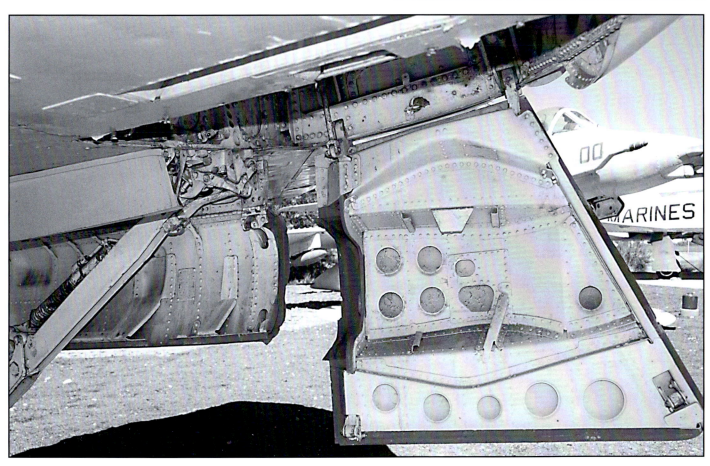

In 1961 the Army issued an invitation to the industry for a light combat jet to be used as a Forward Air Control (FAC) and tactical reconnaissance aircraft. A major requirement was the ability to operate from short and unprepared fields.

Two Douglas A4D-2Ns took part in the demonstration along with a modified Northrop N-156 and an unmodified Fiat G-91. BuNos 148483 and 148490 had an A-3D drag chute added in a long streamlined housing under the tail in place of the tailhook. The main gear were beefed-up and became dual-wheel units. The forward main gear doors were removed and a large bathtub type fairing was added to keep the wheels out of the slipstream.

During the two month test program, the A4D-2N proved to be the clear winner in landing, but no clear winners in take-off and rough field

operations. Douglas proposed its Model 840 which included five weapons pylons. However, no order was forthcoming to the three participants.

Above, Army evaluation A4D-2N, BuNo 148483, with a clear view of the dual main gear and new wheel well fairing. (Gary Verver collection) Below, Army evaluation A4D-2N, BuNo 148490, delivery at Douglas to project pilot Drury Wood. (Harry Gann)

Above, U.S. Army 1961 evaluation of the A4D-2N (BuNo 148483), Northrop N-156 and Fiat G-91 for suitability for a high-speed Forward Air Control (FAC) aircraft that could operate from short unprepared fields. (Tony Chong Collection) Below, A4D-2N, BuNo 148490, in flight with the drag parachute housing installed in place of the tailhook. The forward gear doors were removed and the retracted dual wheels are visible. (Harry Gann) Bottom, the new dual main wheels and new wheel well fairing are evident in this taxi image of BuNo 148490. (Harry Gann)

COCKPIT AND SEAT REMOVED
DURING INVESTIGATION, NO DAMAGE

AFT FUSELAGE
BUCKLED

NOSE GEAR DAMAGED
AFTER NOSE GEAR
COLLAPSED

FUSELAGE PLATING
BROKEN

DROP TANK REMOV
AFTER SALVAGE

PORT MLG
COLLAPSED

NOSE GEAR COLLAPSED
AND NOSE WHEEL SHEARED

The Naval Air Test Center (NATC) is located at NAS Patuxent River, MD, and is responsible for determining an aircraft's suitability for use with the fleet. The A-4C/L versions of the Skyhawk were not subjected to the usual high scrutiny that new aircraft go through at NATC. The improvements aimed at increasing the Skyhawk's combat capability had little effect on the aircraft's handling qualities. Most of the test work revolved around the increased weapons capability.

Above, NATC Service Test (ST) A4D-2N, BuNo 145072, after a landing accident on 25 October 1960. (USN via Angelo Romano) Below, NATC Flight Test (FT) A4D-2N, BuNo 145071, conducting carrier tests on the USS Independence (CVA-62). (USN via Gary Verver)

Above, NATC Weapons Test A4D-2N, BuNo 147826, with Zuni rocket pods during an open house at NAS Patuxent River, MD. (Lionel Paul) Below, NATC Systems Test A-4C, BuNo 145073, in 1971. Tail, nose and outer wing panels were red. (Paul Minert collection) Bottom, Service Test (ST) A-4C, BuNo 149652, with full bomb load. Rudder stripes were red. (Tailhook)

43

NAVAL AIR TEST FACILITY (NATF), LAKEHURST, NJ

The Naval Air Test Facility (NATF) was established at NAS Lakehurst, NJ, in 1958. Their mission was to test and rate aircraft for fleet usage and compatability with existing and new catapult, arresting and barri- er equipment and ship instal- lations of said equipment. NATF was absorbed by the Naval Air Engineering Center (NAEC) in 1977.

Above, NATF A-4C, BuNo 145069, repainted as aircraft 03 on 24 July 1976. (David Ostrowski) Below, NATF A-4C, BuNo 145069, at Andrews AFB, in November 1970. (Jack Morris) Bottom, NATF A-4C, BuNo 145069, in 1971. Triangle on tail was orange/yellow. (Fred Roos)

NAVAL AIR ENGINEERING CENTER (NAEC)

The Naval Air Engineering Center (NAEC) conducted research, development, test and evaluation programs in the field of aerospace structures of aircraft, missile weapons systems, and components. Studies were made on the combined effects of high temperatures and loads on full-scale aircraft and missiles.

Above, NATF A-4C, BuNo 145074, in May 1971. (R. Esposito via Norm Taylor) Below, NAEC A-4L, BuNo 149646, at NAS Lakehurst, NJ, in April 1979. Boomerang on tail was black outlined in Yellow. (Terry Waddington) Bottom, NAEC Lakehurst A-4L, BuNo 149646, at NAS North Island, CA, on 17 September 1974. (Clay Jansson)

NAVAL AIR DEVELOPMENT CENTER (NADC), JOHNSVILLE, PA

Johnsville, PA, was originally Brewster's wartime production plant for SB2A Buccaneers/Bermudas (see Naval Fighters #76). The Navy terminated Brewster's contracts on 1 July 1944 for unsatisfactory performance and took over the field. Specializing in the installation of radar, the Naval Aviation Modification Unit (NAMU) was transferred from Philadelphia to Johnsville.

In 1954, the base housed the Naval Air Development Center (NADC) as part of the Naval Material Command (NMC). NADC's mission was research, design, development, test and evaluation of aeronautical systems and components, and research and development work in aviation medicine.

NADC was divided into eight functional departments:

1.) **Aero Electronic Technology**
2.) **Aerospace Medical Research**
3.) **Aero Mechanics**
4.) **Systems Analysis and Engineering**
5.) **Aero Materials**
6.) **Aerospace Crew Equipment**
7.) **Aero Structures**
8.) **Naval Air Facility**

The Naval Air Facility was responsible for supplying the aircraft and pilots for the various test programs, and the test programs dictated what aircraft were assigned to NADC.

Below, the first A4D-2N built, BuNo 145062, operated as a Johnsville A-4C in April 1965. (Roger Besecker) Bottom, NADC NA-4C, BuNo 145062, at Warminster on 15 May 1971. (Stephen Miller)

Above, NADC A-4C, BuNo 145062, in 1972. Dark blue circle with gold letters on the tail. (Angelo Romano collection) Below, NADC A-4C, BuNo 147680, on 19 May 1973. (Jack Morris) Bottom, NADC NA-4C, BuNo 145062, landing in March 1974. Logo on tail is white outlined in red with a dark blue inner circle and gold letters. (Ron Picciani)

NAF DAHLGREN, VA

NAVAL AEROSPACE RECOVERY FACILITY (NARF)

The Naval Parachute Facility (NPF), later Naval Aerospace Recovery Facility (NARF), is stationed at NAS El Centro, CA. The facility has operated a wide range of Naval aircraft to fullfill its basic mission of the development and testing of aircraft egress systems, primarily rocket ejection seats. In that capacity, NARF operated the second A4D-2N, BuNo 145063, as an NA-4C.

At top, NADC A-4L, BuNo 149646, at NAS Miramar, CA, in April 1976. NADC arrow on the tail was black. (Norm Taylor collection) Above, ex-NATC Systems Test A4D-2N, BuNo 145072, retired to Dahlgren in May 1975. The A4D-2N designation was retained, the intake warning markings were black and HERO on the tail was black outlined in yellow. (Ron Picciani) Below, NARF NA-4C, BuNo 145063, the second A4D-2N built, at El Centro, CA, in 1973. Tail triangle was yellow outlined in blue. (Norm Taylor collection)

NAVAL WEAPON EVALUATION FACILITY (NAVWPNEVALFAC), KIRKLAND AFB

The "Rio Grande Navy" was established in 1949. Naval Aircraft assigned to the Naval Weapons Evaluation Facility (NWEF) at Kirkland AFB, NM, were involved in developing and testing methods of delivering nuclear weapons. Since the Skyhawk was developed around the special weapons mission, it was only natural that it was used at NWEF.

Above, NWEF A-4C, BuNo 145074, at Kirkland AFB in November 1969. Thunderbird logo on the tail was black. Note red Walleye missile with yellow lower wings mounted on the center-line. (Nick Williams collection)

NAVAL MISSILE CENTER (NMC), NAS POINT MUGU, CA

Established in 1946, the Naval Air Missile Test Center was responsible for the operational testing and development of naval missile systems. NAMTC became the Naval Missile Center (NMC) in 1959 and the Pacific Missile Test Center (PMTC) in 1975.

Below, NMC A-4C, BuNo 145071, departs NAS Point Mugu, CA, with ten Mk. 82s and a centerline camera pod. (USN)

NAVAL MISSILE CENTER

Naval Missile Center (NMC) A-4C, BuNo 145067 NMC/067, and A-4B 145034, at NAS Pt. Mugu, CA, with daglo red trim. (Harry Gann) At left, NMC A-4C, BuNo 149654 NMC/81, at NAS Pt. Mugu, CA, on 2 November 1971. (Roy Lock via Norm Taylor) Below, Naval Missile Center (NMC) A-4C, BuNo 145073 NMC/87, at NAS Pt. Mugu, CA, in December 1969. (Duane Kasulka) Bottom, NMC A-4C, BuNo 145067 NMC/89, at NAS Pt. Mugu, CA, in December 1969. Tail of A-4B, BuNo 142847, is in the background. (Harry Gann)

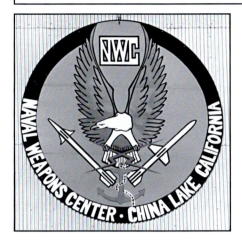

NWC's mission was to develop air-to-air, and air-to-surface missiles, underwater ordnance, and related systems. The single and especially the two-seat A-4s were ideal test vehicles in that it was easy to modify or to substitute nose cones for advanced weapons systems or to install seeker heads.

Above, Walleye being loaded on A-4C, BuNo 148437, at China Lake on 10 February 1964. Loaders (L-to-R) were C.J. Jennings and J.E. Wilcox. (USN) Below, NWC China Lake A-4C, BuNo 147781, shares the runway with a DF-8A. Skyhawk has a centerline-mounted Walleye and its refueling probe removed. (USN) Bottom, NWC China Lake A-4C, BuNo 147680, launching Shrike anti-radar missile which was designed and developed at China Lake. Nose, tail and outer wing panels were red. (USN)

ANTI - SUBMARINE FIGHTER SQUADRON ONE, VSF-1
"WAR EAGLES / WAR HAWKS"

Anti-Submarine Fighter Squadrons were originally conceived to provide four-plane detachments (Dets) to each CVS/ASW carrier. This would give the CVS carriers a limited air defense and combat air patrol ability. For this mission, the Skyhawks were equipped with two wing-mounted Sidewinders and two 20mm cannons. This role was expanded to include a full light attack capability.

VSF-1 was established on 1 July 1965 at NAS Lemoore, CA, and equipped with the A-4B Skyhawk. On 1 April 1967, VSF-1 was split in two and VSF-3 was established.

In August 1967, the squadron re-equipped with A-4C Skyhawks, receiving six that month (BuNos 147708, 147802, 148558, 149497, 149516, and 150598). In September, BuNos 147822, 149532, and 149573 were acquired, followed by 148602 in October and 147779, 149498, and 150581 in November. In 1968, two A-4Cs, BuNos 147728 and 148586, were received in January, three in February (147749, 149583, and 149608), one in March (147765), and one in June (147750). Eleven replacement A-4Cs were acquired in 1969 (BuNos 147710, 147820, 148446, 148449, 148497, 148553, 149505, 149506, 149547, 149551, and 149604) before the draw-down towards disestablishment. Five aircraft were transferred out in November 1969 and nine in December 1969. VSF-1 was disestablished on 1 January 1970.

The squadron deployed its A-4Cs from 30 April 1968 to 17 January 1969 on a Med cruise aboard the USS Independence (CVA-62) as part of CVW-7 and wore the "AG" tail code. Their fourteen aircraft shared the decks with VA-64 and VA-76 A-

4Cs as well as VF-41 (F-4J), VF-84 (F-4J), RVAH-7 (RA-5C), VAH-10 Det 62 (KA-3B), VAQ-33 Det 62 (EA-1F), VAW-124 (E-2A), and HC-2 (UH-2B).

Det 18 provided four A-4Cs for an Atlantic cruise aboard the USS Wasp (CVS-18) from 20 August to 19 December 1969. From 2 September to 11 December 1969, VSF-1 Det 10 deployed aboard the USS Yorktown (CVS-10) until 11 December 1969. They operated in the North Atlantic for NATO exercise Operation Peacekeeper with four A-4Cs wearing "AU" tail codes.

Below, VSF-1 A-4C, BuNo 148356, on the catapult of the USS Independence (CVA-62) in June 1968. (USN) At top right, VSF-1 A-4C, BuNo 147685, operating aboard the USS Independence (CVA-62) on 24 June 1968. (Angelo Romano collection) At right middle, VSF-1 A-4C, BuNo 147750, assigned to the USS Independence (CVA-62) at NAS Alameda, CA, on 14 April 1969. Rudder trim was green. (William Swisher) Bottom right, VSF-1 A-4C, BuNo 148553, assigned to the USS Independence (CVA-62) at NAS Moffett Field, CA. (Fred Roos)

VSF-1

Above, VSF-1 Det 10 A-4C, BuNo 145128, aboard the USS Yorktown (CVS-10) in 1969. Note Sidewinder missile rails on the wing pylons and the Bear silhouette and red star intercept on the nose. (Ginter collection) At left, VSF-1`A-4C, BuNo 148497, aboard the USS Independence (CVA-62) in 1969. Drop tank trim was green. (Ginter collection) Bottom, VSF-1 Det 10 A-4C, BuNo 147710, assigned to the USS Yorktown (CVS-10) on 31 July 1969. Rudder trim was green. VSF-1 Det 10 is written on the dorsal fairing. (William Swisher)

COMPOSITE SQUADRON ONE, VC-1 "BLUE ALIIS", NAS BARBERS POINT, HI

Composite Squadron One (VC-1) was originally established as Utility Squadron One (VU-1) on 20 July 1951. It was redesignated VC-1 on 1 July 1965. A long-time user of the Skyhawk, VC-1 received its first A-4C in March 1969. By the end of April, the squadron was equipped with six A-4Cs, eight A-4Bs, four US-2Cs and one RC-45J. Four F-8Ks, two UH-34Js and one DP-2E were added by July 1969. The amount of A-4Cs topped-out at ten before A-4Es began replacing them in January 1971. By the end of May 1971, all the A-4Cs had been transferred out of VC-1.

Below, VC-1 CO's A-4C, BuNo 148500 UA/00, at NAS Barbers Point, HI, in April 1969. (Nick Williams) Bottom, VC-1 A-4Cs, BuNos 148500 UA/00 and 147823 UA/42, over Oahu on 12 September 1969. Note "Blue Aliis" insignia has been added to the fuselage sides and the double zeros on 148500 were changed to double nuts. (USN)

55

VC-1 NAS Barbers Point montage by Nick Williams: Top, BuNo 147743 UA/42 in April 1969. Above left, 148450 UA/43 in May 1969. Above right, 149606 UA/45 in April 1969, Below, 149550 UA/44 in April 1969. Bottom, 147823 UA/42 in May 1969. The VC-1 A-4Cs only carried black markings unlike the extremely colorful A-4Es and TA-4Js that replaced them and A-4Bs before them.

FLEET COMPOSITE SQUADRON TWO, VC-2 "BLUE TAILS"

Stationed at NAS Oceana with a detachment at NAS Quonset Point and later NAS Cecil Field, Fleet Composite Squadron Two was established on 1 July 1965 when Utility Squadron Two was redesignated. VC-2 initially was equipped with eleven F-8C and four US-2C aircraft. The Blue Tails flew the Crusader until 1971 when they were completely replaced by Douglas A-4 Skyhawks.

VC-2 provided jet and propeller services to the Atlantic Fleet and conducted combat readiness training along the East Coast. VC-2 operated A-4C, A-4E, A-4L, and TA-4J Skyhawks.

The first three squadron A-4Cs were acquired in May-June 1971 and were operated by VC-2 Det Cecil. Det Cecil also operated US-2Cs. After that point in time, maximum strength of A-4Cs grew to ten in 1972 with four US-2Cs. A-4Es were added in May 1973 and TA-4Js in August 1973. In March 1974, two A-4Ls were acquired. The last A-4C was retired in October 1975 and six A-4Ls remained in operation until late 1976.

Below, VC-2 A-4C, BuNo 145118, at NAS Oceana, VA, on 20 June 1973. CAG bird of Commander Fighter Wing One. Tail markings were white and black as was the fuselage stripe. (Frank MacSorley) Bottom, VC-2 A-4C, BuNo 147783, at NAS Miramar, CA, on 26 August 1973. (Bob Lawson)

Above, VC-2 A-4C, BuNo 148469, at NAS Chase Field, TX, on 25 January 1975. (C. Eddy/Norm Taylor collection) Below, VC-2 A-4C, BuNo 148576, at NAS Oceana, VA, in June 1974. (G. Geer/Norm Taylor collection) Bottom, VC-2 A-4L, BuNo 147836, at NAS Oceana, VA, on 17 August 1975. (R. Leader/Craig Kaston collection)

OPERATIONAL TEST AND EVALUATION FORCE FOUR, VX-4 "EVALUATORS"

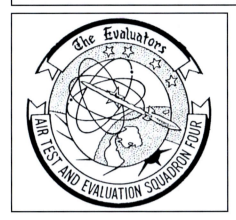

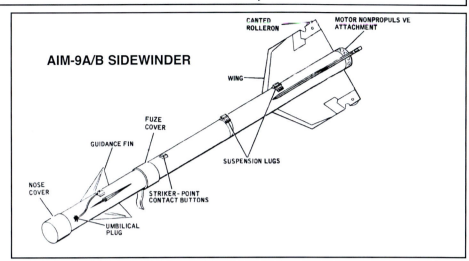

AIM-9A/B SIDEWINDER

Air Development Squadron Four (VX-4) was established on 15 September 1952 at the Naval Missile Center (NMC), NAS Point Nugu, CA. The squadron's mission was to conduct projects dealing with the evaluation of air-launched guided missiles. VX-4's mission evolved into the development of a missile or missile component and its best use as a weapon, to conduct tests and evalua-tions of aircraft weapons systems and support systems in an operational environment, and to develop all-weather intercept tactics for air-launched missiles. VX-4 eventually would operate every version of the Skyhawk in its research and development projects.

Below, VX-4 A-4C, BuNo 149511 XF/40, at NAS Pt. Mugu, CA, while armed with Sidewinders for the air defense role (VSF) aboard ASW carriers. Operational Test and Evaluation Force is lettered on the fuselage side. Tail stripe is dark blue. (USN via Craig Kaston)

FLEET COMPOSITE SQUADRON FOUR DET CECIL, VC-4 "DRAGON FLYERS"

Fleet Composite Squadron Four (VC-4) was established on 1 July 1965 when Utility Squadron Four (VU-4) was redesignated. VC-4 was equipped with F-8 Crusaders which were used to simulate high speed threats to the fleet and provide high speed target services to fleet pilots.

In March 1970, VC-4 Det Cecil received five A-4Cs which operated alongside two F-8Ks and three US-2Cs. By July, only the A-4Cs and US-

2Cs remained to carry out the squadron's mission. VC-4 Det Cecil was operating six A-4Cs and three US-2Cs on 30 April 1971 when it was disestablished.

Below, VC-4 Det Cecil's first A-4C, BuNo 149627, at NAS Oceana, VA, in April 1970. Tail and drop tank trim were red. (William L Swisher)

FLEET COMPOSITE SQUADRON FIVE DET CUBI, VC-5 "CHECKERTAILS"

VC-5 was established on 1 July 1965 when UTRON Five (VU-5) was redesignated. VC-5 was based at NAS Atsugi, Japan, with two detachments at Naha and at Cubi. Originally equipped with F-8 Crusaders, they

provided air services for fleet training. Det Cubi received five A-4Cs in April 1969 to replace its F-8s. These remained until replaced by A-4E/Fs in October 1970.

Below, VC-5 Det Cubi A-4C, BuNo 147752, at Da Nang in September 1970. Rudder was checkered red and yellow. Drop tank flash was red outlined in yellow. (Barry Miller)

AIR DEVELOPMENT SQUADRON FIVE (AIRDEVRON FIVE), VX-5 "VAMPIRES"

Originally known as Air Development Squadron Five, VX-5 was established on 18 June 1951 at NAS Moffett Field, CA. Initially, its mission was to develop and evaluate aircraft tactics and procedures for the delivery of airborne special weapons. In July 1956, the squadron moved to NAF China Lake, CA, thereby enabling the unit to take advantage of the vastly improved ranges and technical facilities at China Lake. In January 1969, the unit's designation was changed to Air Test and Evaluation Squadron Five. The squadron has flown all versions of the A-4 including the C.

Below, VX-5 A-4C, BuNo 145127, at NAS China Lake, CA, in 1965. (Angelo Romano collection) Bottom, VX-5 A-4C, BuNo 148565, in flight with a VX-5 Skyraider. Tail stripe was green. (USN)

FLEET COMPOSITE SQUADRON SEVEN, VC-7 "TALLYHOers / RED TAILS"

Fleet Composite Squadron Seven was established on 1 July 1965 when Utility Squadron Seven was redesignated VC-7 and placed under the command of Commander Fleet Air Miramar. At that time, the squadron had a complement of four DF-8As, fourteen F-8Cs and thirteen A-4Bs. In March 1969, the A-4C replaced the A-4Bs.

VC-7 continued to fly Skyhawks until its disestablishment on 30 September 1980. It would utilize the A-4B, A-4C, A-4E, A-4F, A-4L, TA-4F, and TA-4J Skyhawks.

Below, VC-7 A-4C, BuNo 147708, with a Del Mar target and squadron insignia on the fuselage. The tail was red. (Ginter collection) Below middle, VC-7 CO CDR G.M. Dempsey, Red Tail One's A-4C, BuNo 148548, at Miramar on 31 March 1973. Red Texaco flying horse has been added to the fuselage. (William Swisher) Bottom, VC-7 A-4C, BuNo 147733, at Miramar in October 1972. Note subtle change in the shape of the red tail. (T. Waddington via Kaston)

62

Above, VC-7 A-4C, BuNo 149544, at NAS Miramar, CA, on 28 May 1974. (Bill Curry) Below, VC-7 A-4C, BuNo 147752, at NAS Miramar on 15 September 1974 with a Del Mar target under the wing. (Fred Roos) Bottom, VC-7 A-4L, BuNo 148555, at NAS Miramar, CA, on 12 April 1975. Rudder trim was red. (Bob Lawson)

FLEET COMPOSITE SQUADRON EIGHT, VC-8 "RED TAILS"

Fleet Composite Squadron Eight (VC-8) was established on 18 June 1965 when VU-8 was redesignated VC-8. The unit was stationed at NAS Roosevelt Roads, PR, and flew seven types of aircraft to fulfill its mission. The squadron provided expendable and recoverable targets and flew ECM and interdiction flights against the fleet. In 1976, the squadron took on the adversary mission, too.

The first two A-4Cs were received in May 1969. Thirteen A-4Cs were assigned to VC-8 with the last two being retired in June 1976 after being replaced with TA-4F/Js. These were BuNos: 145132, 147783, 147834, 148304, 148449, 148603, 149489, 149544, 149558, 149586, 150583, 150591, and 150599. The most A-4Cs in use at any one time at VC-8 was nine.

Three A-4Cs were stricken after accidents. These were: 150583 on 14 February 1974, 149586 on 23 May 1974, and 150599 on 6 February 1976.

Above, VC-8 A-4C, BuNo 150599, in June 1972. (R.W. Harrison) Below, VC-8 A-4C, BuNo 147834, bombed up with stylized red hawk applied to the tail in 1969. (Norm Taylor collection)

FLEET COMPOSITE SQUADRON TWELVE, VC-12 "FIGHTING OMARS"

Fleet Composite Squadron Twelve (VC-12) was established on 1 September 1973 at NAF Detroit, MI. It was the first reserve VC squadron and was equipped with nine A-4Ls: BuNos 147669, 147706, 147708, 147827, 149508, 149516, 149518, 149591, and 149623. Only one A-4L, BuNo 145092, was acquired in 1974, on 24 April. Three A-4Ls were received in 1975: 148581 on 7 December, 149540 on 2 September, and 150586 on 29 November. The last A-4L arrived on 3 February 1976.

On 2 July 1975, VC-12 moved to NAS Oceana, VA, where TA-4Js replaced the A-4Ls in 1976. The last A-4L, BuNo 150586, transferred out on 25 January 1977. A-4E/Fs were added in 1983 and the squadron became Composite Fighter Squadron Twelve (VFC-12) on 22 April 1988. In August 1993, the Skyhawks were replaced with Hornets.

Above, VC-12 A-4L, BuNo 147669, in 1974. Forward tail and drop tank stripe were red. Aft tail and drop tank stripe were blue as were the drop tank stars. (Ginter collection) Below, VC-12 A-4L, BuNo 149516, at NAS Oceana, VA, on 25 September 1976. Upper tail stripe was red followed by white and then blue. (Jim Sullivan)

ATTACK SQUADRON TWELVE, VA-12 "FLYING UBANGIS'"

Established on 12 May 1945 as Fighting Bombing Squadron Four (VBF-4) at NAS Alameda, CA, the "Flying Ubangis'" first aircraft was the F4U-4 Corsair. On 15 November 1946, VBF-4 was redesignated Fighter Squadron Two A (VF-2A). In May 1947, the unit converted to F8F-1 Bearcats and a small compliment of F6F-5P Hellcats. VF-2A was redesignated Fighter Squadron 12 (VF-12) in September 1950 when they re-equipped with the F2H-1 Banshee. These were replaced with F2H-2s in December. On 1 August 1955, VF-12 became Attack Squadron Twelve (VA-12) and converted to the F7U-3 Cutlass in December 1955. In April 1957, VA-12 received the A4D-1 Skyhawk. In January 1958, the unit

received the A4D-2 and then the A4D-2N in January 1962.

Seven A-4Cs: BuNos 148580, 145581, 149491, 149499, 149500, 149503, and 149504 were received in January 1962. Four more, BuNos 147806, 147823, 149513, and 147758, were acquired in February and 145078, 147697, and 149607 in August. 149627 was received in September 1962 as a replacement for 148580, which was stricken after an accident on 22 June.

In March 1962, the squadron conducted carrier qualifications aboard the new USS Enterprise (CVAN-65) with their new A-4Cs. This was followed by "Operation Trap" beginning

Above, VA-12 A-4Cs, BuNos 149491 AB/401 and 149503 AB/403, aboard the USS Franklin D. Roosevelt (CVA-42) in 1964. Tail trim was red. (USN) Below, four VA-12 A-4Cs, BuNos 149504 AB/404, 149499 AB/402, 149491 AB/401, and 149500 AB/400, in flight on 28 February 1962. (USN)

on 5 April 1962. It was an evaluation firing of the Bullpup air-to-surface missile for the Chief of Naval Operations. Over one hundred Bullpups were fired and the squadron scored the first measured Bullpup bullseye on 9 April.

VA-12's first A-4C deployment

was aboard the USS Franklin D. Roosevelt (CVA-42) from 14 September 1962 through 22 April 1963 as part of CVG-1. While visiting Athens, Greece, VA-12 personnel painted a school house and installed playground equipment in the small country village of Kalyvia. Ports-of-Call were: Rhodes, Athens, Istanbul, Cannes, Naples, Palermo, Genoa, and Barcelona.

During the summer and fall of 1963, VA-12 sent two fighter support detachments aboard the ASW carriers USS Essex (CVS-9) and the USS Intrepid (CVS-11).

During January through March 1964, training was conducted at Guantanamo Bay, Cuba, aboard the F.D.R. VA-12's second A-4C deployment was from 28 April through 2 December 1964 aboard the F.D.R.

again. During the cruise, the squadron took part in Operation Fairgame II from 13 to 17 May, joint US/UK bilateral exercise the week of 19 June, stood ready as part of the Cypress Evacuation Force from 10 to 31 August, Operation Fallex 4-64 from 23-28 September, and Operation Haystrike 4-64 from 18 to 27 November. The following ports also were visited: Barcelona, Palma, Naples, Malta, Athens, Cannes, Taranto, Messina, Rhodes, Gibraltar, Palermo, Valencia and Poliesa Bay.

The squadron made a short cruise to the Caribbean in February 1965, and then transitioned to the new A-4E Skyhawk at Cecil Field. VA-12 made two F.D.R. deployments with the A-4E before transitioning back to A-4Cs in March 1967. The twelve A-4Cs received in March were: BuNos 145099, 147702, 147744,

Above, VA-12 CAG bird A-4C, BuNo 149600, assigned to the USS Franklin D. Roosevelt (CVA-42) for its 1967-1968 deployment. Tip of rudder was red with a white CVW-1 applied. Rudder tabs top-to-bottom: red, yellow, blue, orange, green, dark blue, maroon, black, and red. (Bob Lawson) Bottom, VA-12 A-4C, BuNo 149585, assigned to the USS Franklin D. Roosevelt (CVA-42) on 9 August 1968. Tail trim was red. (Nick Williams collection)

148480, 148487, 148545, 149503, 149513, 149564, 149566, 149585, and 149600. In April, two more A-4Cs were added, BuNos 147806 and 148591. The final A-4C to be received in 1967 was 149565, acquired on 22 May.

VA-12 deployed its A-4Cs to the

Mediterranean aboard the F.D.R. from 24 August 1967 through 19 May 1968 as part of CVW-1 once more. This was followed by another Med deployment, this time aboard the USS Shangri-La (CVA-38) from 7 January through 29 July 1969 as part of CVW-8 (AJ tail code). LTJG Frank Neuman was Killed on 12 February 1969 during recovery after he ejected as his A-4C went over the side. Ports-of-Call were; Barcelona, Cannes, Naples, Athens, and Malta.

After this cruise, all its aircraft were traded out for freshly refurbished A-4Cs with upgraded engines, dubbed "Super Charlie" by the squadron. These were: BuNos 145097, 145105, 145122, 147681, 147690, 147792, 147803, 147824, 147845, 148464, 148536, 148590, 148601, 149493, 149553, 149556, and 149587. Commanded by CDR Walter Peterson, VA-12 conducted four training cruises during the

months of November, December, January, and February. VA-12 was rated the best bombers in the Air Wing when the pre-deployment ORI was concluded.

The squadron's last A-4C deployment was a war cruise aboard CVA-38 again, from 5 March through 17 December 1970. During the cruise, the squadron lost two A-4Cs operationally with both pilots being recovered safely. BuNo 147803 was lost on 28 April and 149553, flown by LT Danny Flynn, was lost on 6 August 1970. Due to these losses and maintenance issues, five replacements were received during the cruise: 149586 in April, 148609 in May, 147734 in May, 147687 in June, and 147797 in August 1970.

By the time VA-12 had finished its first two line periods, they had dropped over 900,000 lbs of ordnance. Total flight hours for April were

Above, VA-12 A-4C, BuNo 149564, assigned to CO, CDR Richard Fletcher, on 29 September 1969. (J. Wible/Mike Wilson collection) Bottom, VA-12 A-4C, BuNo 147845, assigned to the USS Shangri-La (CVA-38) in September 1969. (J. Wible/Nick Williams collection)

730, averaging over 60 hours per plane and over 36 hours per pilot. Due to weather and transit times, only 535 flight hours were flown in May. By the end of August, 3,611 flight hours were flown, 1,556 day carrier landings and 372 night carrier landings were clocked while 4,582 bombs were dropped. When the "Shang" retired to CONUS, VA-12 had flown nearly 4,000 hours and 2,400 combat sorties

The "Shang" spent 120 days on the line and visited Rio de Janeiro, Subic Bay, DaNang, Yokosuka,

Above, VA-12 A-4C, BuNo 149553 AJ/401, landing at Atsugi on 20 July 1970. Rudder trim was red. (Toyokazu Matsuzaki) At right, VA-12 A-4C, BuNo 148590 AJ/404, at Da Nang in June 1970. (Barry Miller) Below right, VA-12 A-4C, BuNo 149586 AJ/410, from CVA-38 at Atsugi, Japan, on 20 July 1970. (T. Matsuzaki) Bottom, VA-12 A-4C, BuNo 149493 AJ/406, assigned to the USS Shangri-La (CVA-38) taxiis at Atsugi on 20 July 1970. (T. Matsuzaki)

Manila, Hong Kong, Sydney, and Wellington.

After VA-12 returned to CONUS, the squadron, commanded by CDR Daniel Gholson, transferred out its A-4Cs in January 1971 and transitioned to the A-7E Corsair.

FLEET COMPOSITE SQUADRON THIRTEEN, VC-13 "SAINTS"

Above, VC-13 A-4L, BuNo 145122, being towed with a Del Mar target under the left wing in May 1975. (Barry Miller) Below, VC-13 A-4L, BuNo 147825, at NAS Miramar, CA, on 1 May 1975. (Paul Minert collection) Bottom, VC-13 A-4L, BuNo 145092, at NAS New Orleans on 15 June 1975. The hump, tail trim and drop tank arrows were blue. (Robert Mills Jr. via Carig Kaston)

Composite Squadron Thirteen (VC-13) was established on 1 September 1973 with the aircraft and personnel from the disestablished VSF-76 and VSF-86. The NAS New Orleans-based reserve squadron's primary mission was to provide Dissimilar Air Combat Training (DACT) to the fleet. Originally flying the F-8H Crusader, the squadron transitioned to the A-4L Skyhawk in March 1974 and transferred its duty station to NAS Miramar, CA, in February 1976. The A-4Ls were replaced with A-4Es, A-4Fs and TA-4Js. These later were supplemented with F-16Ns. VC-13 was redesignated VFC-13 on 15 April 1988 and the Skyhawks and Falcons were replaced with F/A-18 Hornets in 1993.

VC-13 had ten A-4Ls, eight of which were received in March 1974. These were: BuNos 145122, 147825, 149536, 149551, 149555, 149556, 149607, and 149635. The ninth A-4L was acquired on 24 April 1974 and the tenth on 10 January 1976. The squadron's last A-4L, BuNo 148538, was transferred out on 15 December 1976.

ATTACK SQUADRON FIFTEEN, VA-15 "VALIONS"

VA-15 was originally established as Torpedo Squadron Four (VT-4) on 10 January 1942. Initially equipped with TBD Devastators, the squadron transitioned to TBF/TBM Avengers in August 1942. On 15 November 1946, VT-4 became Attack Squadron Two A (VF-2A) and on 2 August 1948 became Attack Squadron Fifteen (VA-15). They acquired AD Skyraiders on 19 August 1949 and flew the type until September 1965 when A-4s were acquired.

Initially, the squadron received nine A-4Cs. The A-4Cs were traded in during December 1965 and January 1966 for A-4Bs, with the Cs going to units deployed to Vietnam. These A-4Cs were: BuNos 145099,

Above, VA-15 A-4C, BuNo 149607 AK/201, overflies CVS-11 in 1967. (USN via Angelo Romano collection) Bottom, bombed-up VA-15 CAG bird, BuNo 149619, taxiis on the USS Intrepid (CVS-11) off Vietnam in 1967. Note VA-15 AK/201 has a Shrike under its left wing. Tail trim was gold as was background of VA-15 and the squadron insignia. (USN via Mark Aldrich collection)

148480, 148495, 148503, 148516, 148543, 148545, 149611, and 149621. VA-15 made one deployment to Vietnam with its A-4Bs aboard the USS Intrepid (CVS-11) from 4 April to 21 November 1966.

After returning to NAS Cecil Field, FL, VA-15 transitioned back to the A-4C and acquired twelve in December 1966. These were: BuNos 147785, 148466, 148470, 148480, 148484, 148487, 148495, 148503, 148544, 148545, 149529, and 149621. On 14 February 1967, BuNos 149611 (acquired 9 February 1967) and 150600 (acquired 5 January 1967), collided and crashed near MacClenny, FL. The two pilots, LCDR Jerry Tuttle and LTJG Samuel Gerard, Jr., ejected safely and were recovered.

Above, VA-15 A-4C, BuNo 148529 AK/215, taxiis at Atsugi in July 1967. (Angelo Romano collection) Below, VA-15 A-4C, BuNo 149586, being used as a backdrop for a crew photo aboard the USS Intrepid (CVS-11). (USN via Mark Aldrich collection) Bottom, VA-15 A-4C, BuNo 148484 AK/214, on the hanger deck of CVS-11 in 1967. (USN via Mark Aldrich)

Most of these were traded out just before the squadrons second war cruise aboard Intrepid. The following A-4Cs including replacements were flown over Vietnam: 147670, 147803, 148440, 148446, 148466, 148470, 148484, 148528, 148544, 148610, 149493, 149529, 149586, 149607, 149619, and 149621.

VA-15's A-4C war cruise aboard Intrepid was from 11 May through 30 December 1967 while under the command of CDR William Carr. 103 days were spent on the line and five aircraft were lost to enemy actions. The first, shot down by AAA on 30 June 1967, was BuNo 148466 AK/205. The pilot, LT L.O. Cole Jr., ejected but was listed as MIA. A second pilot, LT P.C. Craig, also was listed as missing in action after being shot down on 4 July 1967 in BuNo 148544 AK/208. On 2 August 1967, LT D.W. Thornhill was rescued after being shot down by AAA over the North on a mission to Hon Gai in BuNo 147670 AK/212. Another pilot, LTJG R.W. Gerard, was rescued on 24 August 1967 after being shot down by AAA in BuNo 148440 AK/211. Finally, LCDR P.V. Schoeffel became a POW on 4 October 1967 after being shot down by AAA in BuNo 149619 AK/200.

After returning to Cecil, most of the veteran combat A-4Cs were

Above, VA-15 A-4C, 148543 AK-401, at Douglas Long Beach, in May 1968 just prior to the squadron's CVA-59 deployment. Rudder trim was gold and black and background for VA-15 and squadron insignia was gold. (Harry Gann) Below, VA-15 A-4C, BuNo 149530, traps aboard the USS Forrestal (CVA-59) in 1969. (USN via Angelo Romano collection)

replaced in January 1968. Aircraft on hand were: BuNos 147688, 147696, 147745, 147783, 147830, 148452, 148460, 148463, 148543, 148571, 148594, 148599, 149524, 149530, 149569, and 149638.

Many of these were replaced with refurbished aircraft for the cruise aboard Forrestal. The following aircraft were on hand for that cruise: BuNos 147789, 147792, 147830, 148452, 148459, 148460, 148463, 148543, 148571, 149524, 149530, 149601, and 149628.

The squadron's last deployment was to the MED in their A-4Cs aboard the USS Forrestal (CVA-59) as part of CVW-17 from 22 July 1968 through 29 April 1969. During the cruise, LT Ronald Gerard, Sr. was killed in BuNo 147789 on 18 August 1968 when he ejected inverted too close to the water. Cause of the crash was unknown. On 25 October 1968, LTJG W.A. Harms ejected safely when the engine in BuNo 148459 failed. He was recovered and flown back to CVA-59 by an HC-2 helo.

VA-15 was disestablished on 1 June 1969.

At right, two VA-15 A-4Cs, BuNos 148463 AA/405 and 148571 AA/410, with two VA-152 A-4Bs on CVA-59 in 1969. (USN via Mark Aldrich collection)

73

ATTACK SQUADRON TWENTY - TWO, VA-22 "FIGHTING REDCOCKS"

Attack Squadron Twenty-Two (VA-22) originally was established as Fighter Squadron Sixty-Three (VF-63) on 27 July 1948 at NAS Norfolk, VA. The squadron's first aircraft was the F4U Corsair. These were replaced with F9F-2/5 Panthers in November 1952, which in turn were replaced with F9F-8 Cougars in July 1955.

The squadron's mission changed to that of light attack and its designation was changed to Attack Squadron Sixty-Three (VA-63) in March 1956. In July 1957, the Cougars were replaced with the FJ-4B Fury. Then on 1 July 1959, VA-63 was redesignated Attack Squadron Twenty-Two (VA-22).

In March 1960, they transitioned to the A4D-2 Skyhawk. On 6 October 1961 while stationed at NAS Lemoore, CA, the A4D-2N (A-4C) replaced all but a small number of A4D-2s, which were retained to provide Sidewinder armed DETs on the anti-submarine carriers.

The squadron flew the A-4C until June 1968 when they were replaced with A-4Fs and a limited number of TA-4Fs. On 4 February 1971, the squadron transitioned to the Vought A-7E Corsair II.

Above, VA-22 A-4C, BuNo 147759 NE/223, assigned to the USS Midway (CVA-41) making a practice Mighty Mouse missile attack off Vietnam in June 1965. (USN) Bottom, VA-22 A-4C, BuNo 148578 NE/305, while assigned to the USS Midway (CVA-41) in 1963. Fin tip was red. (Ginter collection)

VA-22 deployed its A-4Cs aboard the USS Midway (CVA-41) from 6 March to 23 November 1965 for the

Above, VA-22 A-4C, BuNo 149490 NE/231, piloted by LTJG Tom Murray pulling forward to the catapult for a refueling mission over Vietnam on 26 May 1965. (USN) Below, fire crew spraying foam under the belly of VA-22 A-4C, BuNo 148587, aboard the USS Midway (CVA-41) in the fall of 1965. (USN)

squadron's first war cruise to Vietnam. The CO, CDR Donald Wyand, lost four aircraft to enemy action over Vietnam. The first, BuNo 149507 NE/204, was lost on 20 April when LT Phillip N. Butler was downed by the blast of his own Mk. 81 bombs. He successfully ejected and became a prisoner of war. On 3 June, LT Raymond P. Ilg (later VADM) was on an armed road recon mission over northern Laos when he was downed in BuNo 148577 NE/2?? by AAA. After avoiding capture for three days, he was recovered by helicopter. The third loss was BuNo 148564 NE/207 on 13 August, also downed by AAA. It was piloted by LT W.E. Newman who was rescued uninjured. LTJG R.M.

Brunhaver was shot down in BuNo 149490 NE/211 by AAA on 24 August, ejected, was captured, and became a POW.

The squadron's second war cruise was aboard the USS Coral Sea (CVA-43) from 29 July 1966 to 23 February 1967. During this deployment, CDR Henry D. Arnold, CO of VA-22, was awarded the Silver Star for his actions during a strike against the Haiphong surface-to-air missile support facility. Six A-4Cs were lost during the cruise. The first, BuNo 148488 NE/200, was lost on 17 September when it was shot down by AAA over North Vietnam. The pilot, LTJG R.A. Hegstrom, was rescued.

Above, VA-12 A-4C, BuNo 148567 NE/209, assigned to the Midway in 1965 with a buddy store on the center pylon. (Clay Jannsson) Bottom, VA-22 A-4C, BuNo 148578 NE/225, from CVA-41 at NAS Cubi Point, PI, in November 1965. (USN via Dave Ekstrand)

BuNo 147737 NE/224 was lost to AAA over the north on 4 October when LCDR J.D. Burns became a POW. On 11 November, BuNo 147718 was lost at sea and its pilot was recovered. LTJG W.T. Arnold went MIA in BuNo 148496 NE/222 when he failed to return from a mission on 17 November after being shot

The fighting cocks from the Midway

76

down by AAA. Another A-4C, BuNo 149641, was lost at sea and the pilot was recovered on 27 December 1966. The last aircraft lost during the cruise was BuNo 150584 NE/223. It was flown by LTJG J.M. Hays who was recovered after

Above, VA-22 A-4C, BuNo 148458 NE/222, assigned to the USS Coral Sea (CVA-43) on 12 March 1967. (Harry Gann) Below, VA-22 A-4C CAG bird, BuNo 148488 NE/00, prepared for launch from the USS Coral Sea (CVA-43) in 1966. (USN)

being downed by AAA on 4 January 1967.

The squadron's third war cruise was aboard the USS Ranger (CVA-61) from 4 November 1967 to 25 May 1968. Unlike its previous two war cruises, VA-22 lost no aircraft while deployed aboard Ranger to South East Asia. During the deployment, CVA-61 was diverted to the Sea of Japan from 23 January to 5 March 1968 in response to the North Korean capture of the USS Pueblo AGER-2.

Above, VA-22 A-4C, BuNo 149555 NE/201, at Edwards AFB, CA, on 20 May 1967. (Nick Williams) Below, VA-22 A-4C, BuNo 147815, assigned to the USS Ranger (CVA-61) at NAS Alameda, CA, on 28 October 1967. (Bob Lawson) Bottom, VA-22 A-4C, BuNo 149630 NE/216, at NAS Lemoore, CA, in 1968. Fuselage stripe and tail markings were in medium blue. (Harry Gann)

ATTACK SQUADRON THIRTY - FOUR, VA-34 "BLUE BLASTERS"

Attack Squadron Thirty-Four (VA-34) was originally established as VF-20 on 15 October 1943 with F6F-3 Hellcats as a unit of Air Group 20 at NAS San Diego, CA. F8F-1 Bearcats replaced the Hellcats in April 1946 and the squadron was redesignated VF-9A on 15 November 1946. On 12 August 1948, VF-9A was redesignated VF-91 and F8F-2s replaced the F8F-1s in December 1948. On 15 February 1950, VF-91 became VF-34 and received Grumman F9F-2 Panthers in November. F2H-2 Banshees replaced the Panthers in February 1952 and the squadron was redesignated Attack Squadron 34 on 1 July 1955. In October 1955, VA-34 received its first Vought F7U-3 Cutlass, which was operated until the A4D-1 Skyhawk began arriving in March 1957. In October 1958, the A4D-2 arrived and in July 1962 VA-34 transitioned to the A-4C Skyhawk.

During the Cuban Missile Crisis from 26 October to 18 November 1962, the squadron boarded the USS Enterprise (CVAN-65) at sea to augment Air Wing Six in support of the quarantine. This mission continued from 18 to 26 November when VA-34 transferred to the USS Independence (CVA-62).

The first A-4C deployment was aboard the USS Saratoga (CVA-60) from 29 March through 25 October 1963 to the Med and the North Atlantic. On 15 August, a VF-31 F-3B crashed into a Skyhawk taxiing on deck and a fire ensued that engulfed seven aircraft. In that fire, two VA-34 A-4Cs were lost, BuNos 148476 and 149592.

In December 1963, a detachment of Sidewinder-equipped A-4Cs were deployed aboard the ASW carrier Intrepid and in January 1964 a second Det was operating from the Randolph.

Below, VA-34 A-4C, BuNo 149603 AC/312, aboard the USS Saratoga (CVA-60) in 1963. Tail trim and fuselage checkmark were medium blue. (USN)

At left, VA-34 A-4C CAG bird in front of VA-34, BuNo 149601, aboard the Saratoga on 21 October 1965. (USN via Mark Aldrich) Bottom, VA-34 A-4C, BuNo 149593 AC/305, seen taxiing at the Paris Air Show on 19 June 1965 while assigned to the USS Saratoga (CVA-60). (Capt Humblot via Norm Taylor)

squadron sailed aboard the USS Intrepid (CVS-11) for its first war deployment. Four aircraft were lost to enemy action during the cruise. The first was piloted by LCDR E.H. Martin who became a POW after punching-out of BuNo 149603 AK/312 on 9 July 1967. Then, on 18 September, a SAM downed LCDR S.H. Hawkins, who was recovered in BuNo 149590 AK/301. AAA bagged BuNo 148566 AK/314 on 7 November with the pilot, LTJG M.A. Krebs, being recovered. Finally, BuNo 149546 AK/306 was lost to a SAM on 17 November. The pilot, W.D. Key, was captured and became a POW. The squadron returned to CONUS on 30 December 1967.

Two more Med cruises were conducted aboard CVA-60 with the A-4C. These were from 28 November 1964 through 12 July 1965 and 11 March 1966 through 26 October 1966. Between these two cruises, on the night of 28 September 1965, LTJG Calvin C. Mahnke in BuNo 149598 and LTJG Robert F. Silvestri in 150590 collided and died six miles south of Cecil Field in an IFR approach when one pilots radio failed.

On 11 May 1967, under the command of CDR Richard A. Wigent, the

On 6 March 1968, LCDR

Above, VA-34 A-4C, BuNo 149640 AK/311, while assigned to the USS Intrepid (CVS-11) in September 1967. Fin tip and fuselage checkmark were medium blue. (Wayne Mutza via Mark Aldrich) At right, VA-34 A-4C, BuNo 149624 AK/315, at NAS Alameda, CA, in February 1968. Drawing on the tail was labeled the Galloping Ghost. (Tailhook collection) Bottom, VA-34 A-4Cs from the USS Intrepid (CVS-11) on 23 July 1967 while at NAS Atsugi, Japan. (Toykazu Matsuzaki)

Hawkins in BuNo 148520 and LTJG J.M. Gill in 149626 were part of a

At left, VA-34 A-4C CAG bird, BuNo 148483 AA/300, over Forrestal in 1968. (Tailhook collection) Below, VA-34 A-4C, BuNo 148316 AA/316, in May 1968 with CVW-17's AA tail code as used during the squadron's 1968-69 deployment aboard the USS Forrestal (CVA-59). (Harry Gann) Bottom, VA-34 A-4C, BuNo 148304 AA/304, taxiing on the deck of the USS Forrestal (CVA-59) in 1968. (Tailhook collection)

twenty-two plane Alpha Strike out of Fallon, NV, when Gill collided with Hawkins. 148520 lost four feet of the left wing and its drop tank and the aircraft went into a violent left spin. Hawkins ejected safely and Gill landed the damaged 149626 at NWC China Lake.

The squadron's last A-4C deployment was aboard the USS Forrestal (CVA-59) on a cruise to the Mediterranean from 22 July 1968 through 29 April 1969. Two aircraft were lost during the cruise. The first was BuNo 149499, lost at sea on 26 January 1969. The pilot, LTJG N.S.

Kobylk was recovered by helicopter. On 22 March 1969, LT James Gill ejected from BuNo 147746 after a flame-out and was recovered by helicopter. One month after returning to CONUS, on 29 May 1969, the squadron was disestablished.

ATTACK SQUADRON THIRTY - SIX, VA-36 "ROADRUNNERS"

Attack Squadron Thirty-Six (VA-36) started out as Fighter Squadron One Hundred Two (VF-102) on 1 May 1952 with FG-1Ds assigned. The squadron received F9F-5 Panthers in October 1955 and was redesignated VA-36 on 1 July 1955. The Roadrunners transitioned to F9F-8/8B Cougars on 2 November 1956 and later added two-seat F9F-8Ts. The A4D-2 was acquired on 11 September 1958 and in turn was replaced with the A4D-2N (A-4C) on 21 March 1961. VA-36 was disestablished on 1 August 1970.

VA-36 and their A-4Cs were assigned to CVG-3 aboard the USS Saratoga (CVA-60) in 1961 when the Sara was dispatched to the waters near Cuba and put on alert during the

Bay of Pigs invasion from 5 July to 22 August. On 5 November, LTJG Richard O. Benoit ejected from BuNo 147846 after an engine failure on approach to NAS Jacksonville, FL. In 1963, VA-36 received a flight safety award while flying over 5,000 hours and 1,337 carrier landings.

Four more deployments aboard Saratoga followed: 28 November 1961 to 11 May 1962, to the Med; 3 December to 21 December 1962, to the Caribbean; 29 March to 25 October 1963, to the Med; and 28 November 1964 to 12 July 1965, to the Med.

On 15 August 1963, an F-3B crashed into VA-36 A-4C, BuNo 148554, destroying it and damaging

Above, VA-36 A-4C, BuNo 148545 AC/612, on CVA-60 in 1963. (USN) Bottom, VA-36 A-4C, BuNo 147733 AC/612, at NAS Cecil Field, FL, on 14 July 1964 while assigned to the USS Saratoga (CVA-60). Tail trim was black. (William T. Larkins)

five other aircraft on CVA-60. Another aircraft was lost on 9 March 1964 when LTJG W.R. Alcorn safely ejected from BuNo 148574 near Jacksonville, FL. The A-4C crashed into a wooded area and burned.

VA-36 deployed their A-4Cs to Vietnam aboard the USS Enterprise (CVAN-65) as part of CVW-9 from 26 October 1965 through 21 June 1966.

At left, VA-36 A-4C, NG/707, landing aboard the USS Enterprise (CVAN-65) in 1966. (USN) Bottom, VA-36 A-4C, BuNo 147764 NG/710, being used as a backdrop for VA-36's pilots aboard Enterprise in 1964 off Vietnam. (USN)

Med aboard the USS America (CVA-66) from 10 January through 20 September 1967. During this cruise VA-36 provided air cover for the USS Liberty (AGTR-5) when it came under attack by Israeli forces.

Another war deployment of VA-36 was conducted aboard the USS Intrepid (CVS-11) as part of CVW-10 from 4 June 1968 through 8 February 1969. On this cruise, no aircraft were lost to enemy action, but one, BuNo 148470, was lost at sea operationally on 20 August 1968. The pilot, LTJG Richard T. Holden, ejected and was recovered safely.

On 31 July 1969, while on a practice dive bombing mission at Pinecastle, FL, LCDR Alan Everest Hospes ejected from BuNo 149538 after its engine quit. His chute failed to open and he fell to his death in the swamp.

Four aircraft were lost during the cruise. The first loss was A-4C, BuNo 148305 NG/705, on 22 December 1965 over North Vietnam. AAA was responsible for LTJG W.R. Alcorn becoming a POW. LTJG S.B. Jordan lost BuNo 147753 NG/713 to his own Snakeye bomb over Laos on 14 January 1966. He was recovered safely. On 20 March 1966, CDR J.A. Mulligan also became a POW when he was shot down by AAA in BuNo 148313 NG/703. Finally, BuNo 147762 NG/712, was downed by AAA on 23 May 1966. ENS K.W. Leuffen was recovered safely. During the cruise, VA-36 flew 2,512 sorties for a total of 4,735 flight hours.

The squadron was re-assigned to CVW-8 (AJ tail code) on 15 July 1966, followed by CVW-6 (AE tail code) on 1 September 1966. As part of CVW-6, VA-36 deployed to the

At right, VA-36 A-4C, BuNo 147709 NG/716, launching from CVAN-65 in 1966. (USN K31272) Bottom, during VA-36's CVAN-65 war cruise, some squadron aircraft took part in a camouflage test. Here VA-36 A-4C, NG-703, taxiis in washable lizard green paint. In the background, VA-36 (707, 712, 711), VA-76 (513, 504), and VA-93 (301, 306) Skyhawks line the deck. (USN K31578)

The squadron's final cruise was aboard the USS Forrestal (CVA-59) from 2 December 1969 through 8 July 1970 to the Mediterranean. On 8 January 1970, LT Rodney E. Kuehn

Above, VA-36 A-4C CAG bird, BuNo 149539 AK/500, at Long Beach, CA, while assigned to the USS Intrepid (CVS-11) in February 1969. The tail and drop tank trim and the Roadrunner on the fuselage were green. (Harry Gann) At left, VA-36 A-4Cs, BuNos 148470 AK/520 and 148610 AK/510, with hooks down returning to CVS-11 off the coast of Vietnam in 1968. (USN) Bottom, VA-36 A-4C CAG bird, BuNo 149558 AK/501, at Long Beach, CA, while assigned to the USS Intrepid (CVS-11) in February 1969. (Harry Gann)

was killed during night operations when he flew into the water about four miles from

Above, VA-36 A-4Cs BuNos 147809 AE/516, 149520 AE/510, 149563 AE/503, 147747 AE/504 from the USS America (CVA-66) in 1967. (USN) At right, VA-36 A-4C, BuNo 149492 AA/514, aboard CVA-59 in 1970. (Ginter collection) Bottom, VA-36 A-4C, BuNo 149519 AA/511, at Forbes AFB, KS, while assigned to the USS Forrestal (CVA-59) in November 1969. The shape of the fuselage Roadrunner image was changed for this cruise. (Jerry Geer via Norm Taylor collection)

CVA-59 in BuNo 149519. A search of the area found a drop tank, pilot's helmet and minor debris.

ATTACK SQUADRON FORTY - THREE, VA-43 "CHALLENGERS"

Attack Squadron Forty-Three (VA-43) was established on 1 July 1959 when VF-21 was redesignated VA-43. Initially, the squadron provided replacement pilot training for both the F11F-1 and A4D-1. VA-43 only trained eight Tiger pilots before retiring the F11F-1s. The squadron took on a new mission which was to take over the instrument training mission from VA-44. For this mission, TF-9Js were added to the squadron's complement of aircraft. A4D-2s were added beginning on 17 April 1959 and A4D-2Ns (A-4Cs) beginning on 26 February 1960. By 30 September 1960, the squadron had 10 A4D-1s, 11 A4D-2s, and 9 A4D-2Ns, for replacement pilot training and 21 F9F-8Ts for instrument training. A-4Es were added later and in February 1965 the A-4s were transferred out and the squadron was devoted exclusively to instrument training. VA-43 was redesignated VF-43 on 1 June 1973.

Below, VA-43 A-4C, BuNo 148521 AD/303, with black tail trim. (Tailhook)

ATTACK SQUADRON FORTY - FOUR, VA-44 "HORNETS"

VA-44 was established as Fighter Squadron Forty-Four on 1 September 1950. As VF-44, the squadron operated the F4U-5, F4U-4 and the F2H-2. On 1 January 1956, VF-44 was redesignated VA-44, and began receiving F9F-8 Cougars. In January 1958, the squadron began receiving F9F-8Ts and in February A4D-1s began arriving in preparation for becoming the East Coast Replacement Training Squadron (RAG) for the new A4D-1 Skyhawks. On 1 June, the squadron officially became the RAG. Also in June, TV-2 and T-28B aircraft were acquired to help fulfill VA-44's mission.

The new mission involved flight training for pilots and maintenance training for enlisted personnel prior to their posting to their respective fleet A4D squadrons. VA-44 also was responsible for instrument training for the East Coast. On 8 August 1958, the first A4D replacement pilot graduated from VA-44.

In September 1958, the A4D-2 began replacing the A4D-1s. Then, in January 1959, the squadron started receiving AD-5/6 Skyraiders, and the expanded responsibility of providing replacement training on this aircraft, too. On 9 February 1960, the A4D-2N (A-4C) started replacing the earlier A4D-2s and on 15 February 1963 the Skyraider training ceased as VA-45 was formed to take over this function. On 18 February, VA-44 changed duty stations from NAS Jacksonville, FL, to NAS Cecil Field, FL. The newer A-4E arrived in October 1964 and TA-

Above, VA-44 A-4C, BuNo 147688, landing on CVS-36 in 1970. (Tailhook) Below, VA-44 A-4Cs with BuNo 147688 AD/422 in the foreground at NS Roosevelt Roads, PR, in 1970. (Tailhook) Bottom, VA-44 A-4C, BuNo 147790 AD/414, at NAS Dallas, TX, on 4 May 1968. Fin tip was red. (Fred Roos)

4F Skyhawks began replacing the TF-9Js on 3 August 1966. The squadron received A-4Fs in November 1969 and A-4Ls in December. The squadron was disestablished on 1 May 1970.

ATTACK SQUADRON FORTY - FIVE, VA-45 "HORNETS"

VA-45 was established on 15 February 1963 to take over the replacement pilot training for the A-1 Skyraiders. The squadron adopted the nickname and insignia of the previous VA-45. VA-45 was assigned to Replacement Training Carrier Air Wing Four (RCVW-4). Skyraider training was short-lived with their replacement by TF-9J Cougars in 1964 when they became an instrument training squadron. The Cougars lasted until 1968 when they were completely replaced by Skyhawks. In June 1970, the RCVW Wings were disestablished and the squadrons became known as Fleet Readiness Squadrons (FRS). The Blackbirds flew a wide variety of A-4 Skyhawks and were developed into yet another adversary squadron, being redesignated Fighter Squadron Forty-Five (VF-45) in October 1985.

During the Vietnam War, the USS Intrepid, a CVS, was impressed into service as a limited CVA. It conducted three war cruises with VSF and fleet VA squadrons embarked. After these cruises concluded, the Intrepid still required a Det of combat aircraft for protection and VA-45 fulfilled this need. They did it with A-4Cs from Det II and with humpback A-4Es from Det I. This requirement lasted into 1973.

A-4Cs assigned to VA-45 were: 145106, 147698 AU/661, 148447, 148601, 148609, 149498 AU/662, and 149558 AU/663.

Above, VA-45 Det II A-4C, BuNo 147698 AU/661, aboard CVS-11 in 1971. Fin tip, fuselage and drop tank trim were black. (Ginter collection) Below, VA-45 Det II A-4C, BuNo 149498 AU/662, aboard the USS Intrepid (CVS-11) in 1971. Note Sidewinder rail mounted on the wing pylon. (Ginter collection) Bottom, VA-45 Det II A-4C, BuNo 149558 AU/663, aboard CVS-11 in 1971. (Ginter collection)

ATTACK SQUADRON FORTY - SIX, VA-46 "CLANSMEN"

Attack Squadron Forty-Six was established on 24 May 1955 at NAS Cecil Field, FL. Their first aircraft was the Grumman F9F-5 Panther, which was replaced with F9F-8 Cougars one month later. After two cruises with the Cougars, VA-46 began receiving the A4D-2 Skyhawk in March 1958. These in turn were replaced with A4D-2Ns (A-4Cs) on 29 August 1960.

The squadron's first deployment with A4D-2Ns was from 2 February through 15 May 1961 to the Mediterranean as part of CVG-10 aboard the USS Shangri-La (CVA-38). In April, live firings of the Bullpup missile were conducted by CO CDR H.J. Tate, LCDR C.Y. Dellinger, LCDR C.R. Long, LT W.H. Fleischmann, LT J.H. Kirkpatrick, LT W.H. Byng, and LTJG J.L. Buckley.

The squadron then made three more A4D-2N/A-4C deployments aboard CVA-38 as part of CVG-10. These were: from 7 February to 28 August 1962, from 1 October 1963 to 23 May 1964, and from 10 February to 20 September 1965. All three were cruises to the Med. The final A-4C deployment was as part of CVG-3 aboard the USS Saratoga (CVA-60)

from 11 March to 26 October 1966.

In January 1967, the A-4E was acquired which it flew until September when A-4Bs were received to replace the eleven A-4Es lost in the CVA-59 fire the previous month. VA-46 transitioned to the Vought A-7B Corsair II in May through November 1968. The squadron continued to fly the A-7 until its disestablishment on 30 June 1991.

Below, one of the first two AD4-2Ns received on 29 August 1960, BuNo 147741 AB/401, was assigned to VA-46's CO, CDR Hugh J. Tate. At the time, the squadron was assigned to CVG-1 aboard the USS Franklin D. Roosevelt CVA-42. A Scotish Tartan design was used on the tail and fuselage stripe. Photo taken at NAS Cecil Field, FL, on 21 September 1960. (USN)

Above, VA-46 A-4C, BuNo 147726 AK/502, refuels from VA-46 A-4C, BuNo 148536 AK/508 over the Med. (USN) Below, VA-46 A-4C, BuNo 150596 AK/509, at NAS New York on 6 November 1965. (Abbott Hafter) Bottom, VA-46 A-4Cs BuNos 147741 AK/501, 147748 AK/507, 147766 AK/506, and 148575 AK/500 over the USS Shangri-La (CVA-38) in June 1962. (USN)

ATTACK SQUADRON FIFTY - FIVE, VA-55 "WARHORSES"

VA-55 originally was established as Torpedo Squadron Five (VT-5) on 15 February 1943. The squadron flew the Grumman Avenger throughout the war in the Pacific. VT-5 was redesignated Attack Squadron Six A (VA-6A) on 15 November 1946 and then Attack Squadron Fifty-Five on 16 August 1948. The TBMs were exchanged for AD-1 Skyraiders on 18 June 1949. VA-55 flew the AD-1 and AD-4 during the Korean War and operated the AD-6 and AD-7 until November 1957 when they received the FJ-4B Fury. The A4D-2 arrived in March 1959 and the A4D-

Above, VA-55 A-4Cs on CVA-14 on 18 January 1963. (Mark Aldrich collection) Below, VA-55 A-4C, BuNo 148596 NF/503, at NAS Miramar, CA, in April 1962. Fin tip is green checkerboard and wing tanks have green trim. (Tailhook) Bottom, VA-55 A-4C CAG bird, BuNo 149551 NF/00, in 1963. (Clay Jansson)

Above, VA-55 A-4C CAG bird, NK/500, with CVW-14 NK tailcode while assigned to the USS Constellation in 1967. Tail trim was green. (Tailhook) Below, VA-55 A-4C, BuNo 147710 NK/515, in flight in 1967 while armed with a Shrike. (USN) Bottom, chewed-up vertical fin on VA-55 A-4C CAG bird, BuNo 147678 NK/500, in 1968. (Tailhook)

2N/A-4C in January 1962.

VA-55 deployed to the Western Pacific in their A-4Cs aboard the USS Ticonderoga (CVA-14) as part of CVG-5 from 3 January to 15 July 1963. During the cruise, on 2 May 1963, LTJG Frederick W. Hamilton crashed during an attempted emergency landing aboard CVA-14. Due to a cracked landing gear, BuNo 149602, crashed into the barricade and burst into flames. Hamilton was rescued uninjured and the aircraft was stricken.

After returning to CONUS, VA-55 transitioned to the A-4E in July 1963 and conducted a war cruise aboard CVA-14 in 1964 and aboard CVA-61 in 1964-65. On return to the US, due to shortages of A-4Es, VA-55 transitioned back to A-4Cs for their third war cruise aboard the USS Constellation (CVA-64). The deployment was from 29 April through 4 December 1967. No aircraft were lost to enemy action during the cruise but one A-4C, BuNo 149632 NK/500, was lost operationally on 2 August 1967. LCDR William M. Shewchuk ejected safely five miles from CVA-64 following his launch .

In December 1967/January 1968, the A-4F replaced the aging A-4Cs. VA-55 was disestablished on 12 December 1975.

ATTACK SQUADRON FIFTY - SIX, VA-56 "CHAMPIONS"

Attack Squadron Fifty-Six (VA-56) was established on 4 June 1956 at NAS Miramar, CA. The squadron's first aircraft was the Grumman F9F-3 Panther, which was replaced one month later with F9F-8B Cougars. VA-56 transitioned to the FJ-4B Fury on 29 May 1958. A4D-1 Skyhawks replaced the FJ-4B in December 1958 and the A4D-2 replaced the -1s in April 1959. Three deployments aboard the USS Ticonderoga (CVA-14) were made with the A4D-2s before they were replaced with A-4Es on 15 July 1963. In July 1966, A-4Cs replaced the A-4Es for one cruise with the squadron receiving A-4Es again in August 1967. In January 1969 Vought's A-7 Corsair replaced the Skyhawks. The squadron was disestablished on 31 August 1986.

On 18 August 1966, LCDR Arthur K. Tyszkiewicz ejected safely from BuNo 148570 during a bombing/strafing flight from NAS Lemoore, CA. During his second strafing run, the hydraulic system and fire warning lights came on and stayed on. He ejected at approximately 2,500 feet.

VA-56's only A-4C combat deployment was aboard the USS Enterprise (CVAN-65) from 19 November 1966 through 6 July 1967. Three aircraft were lost during the cruise. BuNos 145087 and 147724 went down after a mid-air on 14 January 1967 with one pilot, LTJG Karl A. Vogelgro III, being rescued and LCDR Tyszkiewicz being killed.

Above, VA-56 A-4C, BuNo 148603 NG/402, at NAS North Island, CA, in July 1967. (Duane Kasulka) Below, VA-56 CAG bird A-4C, BuNo 147683 NG/500, on 10 September 1966. Rudder trim was red as was shadow trim on NG/500. (Harry Gann) Bottom, VA-56 A-4C, BuNo 149644 NG/514, at NAS Lemoore, CA, on 10 September 1966. (Harry Gann)

The third loss was the squadron CO, CDR P.W. Sherman, who was downed by a SAM on 10 June 1967 in BuNo 145145 NG/406. CDR Ernest R. Semour replaced Sherman as CO on 14 July.

ATTACK SQUADRON SIXTY - FOUR, VA-64 "BLACK LANCERS"

Attack Squadron Sixty-Four (VA-64) was established at NAS Oceana, VA, on 1 July 1961 with A4D-2N (A-4C) Skyhawks.

VA-64 Det 48 was formed on 28 December to provide air defense capability for the USS Wasp (CVS-18). Four A-4Bs were added to the squadron in January/February 1962 for this purpose. They were operated aboard Wasp from 17 February through 17 June 1962. In April 1962, the designation was changed VA-64 Det 18B.

Meanwhile, VA-64's A-4Cs were assigned to the USS Independence (CVA-62) and CVG-1. As such, the squadron deployed on 18 November to 5 December 1962 in response to the Cuban Missile Crisis. On 5 December, the squadron switched decks to the USS Enterprise (CVAN-65) and CVG-6 and continued the quarantine. The Enterprise then deployed to the Med from 6 February to 4 September 1963.

A second CVAN-65 deployment, a world cruise, was conducted from 8 February to 3 October 1964. The ship operated near Cyprus in March 1964 to keep tabs on a conflict between

Above, VA-64 A-4Cs, BuNos 148609 AF/612, 148606 AF/611, 148579 AF/607, and 148552 AF/604, on Enterprise in January 1962. AF tail code was replaced with AE tail code in October 1962. Tail and fuselage trim was black. (Vought) Bottom, VA-64 A-4Cs, BuNos 148516 AE/309 and 149618 AE/301, assigned to the USS Enterprise (CVAN-65) on 25 March 1965. (USN via Mark Aldrich)

Turkish and Greek Cypriots. On 27 March, LCDR George E. LeBlanc was rescued after he broke the nose gear of BuNo 149613 AE/303 on

Above, VA-64 A-4C, BuNo 149617 AE/305, traps aboard Enterprise in 1964. (USN) At right, VA-64 A-4C, BuNo 149619 AE/602, on 24 April 1965. (USN) Bottom, VA-64 A-4C, BuNo 147801, prepares for launch from the USS America (CVA-66) on 26 June 1965. (USN)

landing and skidded off the angled deck. He had face and left hand lacerations and a broken right leg. VA-64's LTJG Tucker Taylor became the Enterprise's first "Triple Centurion" during this cruise. On 31 July 1964, the Enterprise left the Med to complete Operation Sea Orbit, the first cir-

Above, VA-64 pilots aboard the USS America (CVA-66) in 1966. (USN) Below, VA-64 A-4C, BuNo 148598 AG/606, aboard the USS Independence (CVA-62) in 1969. AG and 606 were shadowed in red. (Ginter collection) Bottom, VA-64 A-4C, BuNo 147733 AG/610, in 1969. Tail and drop tank trim was black. (Duane Kasulka)

cumnavigation of the world by a nuclear task force.

In 1965, the Air Wing was reassigned to the USS America (CVA-66) for a Med cruise from 30 November 1965 to 10 July 1966. On 16 June 1966, LT Benjamin R. Partin was lost when he crashed off the port bow after a catapult shot in BuNo 147801.

Another CVA-66 Med deployment was conducted from 10 January to 20 September 1967. On 8 June 1967, VA-64 A-4Cs were launched as part of a strike group in response to the Israeli attack on the USS Liberty (AGTR-5). The aircraft were recalled after the Israelis claimed their attack was a mistake. LTJG C.J. Kelaghan ejected from BuNo 147811 with a broken right arm and was recovered on 27 July 1967.

VA-64 was reassigned to CVW-7 in late 1967 and conducted two deployments aboard the USS Independence (CVA-62). The first cruise was to the Mediterranean from 30 April 1968 through 27 January 1969. During the cruise in November 1968, the squadron provided an A-4C, two pilots and seven enlisted men to augment the VSF-1 Det aboard the Wasp. The second CVA-62 deployment was to the North Atlantic from 3 September through 9 October 1969.

VA-66 began life when Fighter Squadron Six Hundred Seventy-One (VF-671) was re-established on 1 February 1951 at NAS Atlanta, GA. The squadron's F4U Corsairs were replaced with F8F Bearcats after VF-671 transferred to NAAS Oceana. F9F-5 Panthers replaced the Bearcats in late 1952 and on 4 February 1953 VF-671 became Fighter Squadron Eighty-One (VF-81). In May 1954, VF-81 became the first fleet squadron to equip with the Chance Vought F7U-3 Cutlass. VF-81 was redesignated VA-81 on 9 April 1955 and F9F-8 Cougars began

replacing the F7U-3s in September 1956. In March 1958, the squadron transitioned to the Douglas A4D-1 Skyhawk. The A4D-2 arrived in June 1959 and was replaced by A4D-2Ns (A-4Cs) in March 1961. In October 1970, the Skyhawks were replaced with Vought A-7E Corsairs and the squadron was disestablished on 31 March 1987.

A three-week training period to the Caribbean near the Dominican Republic was conducted in June 1961. This was followed in July with exercises with the Second Fleet off

Above, CAG bird A4D-2N, BuNo 148455 AF/00, at NAS Oceana on 20 May 1961. Rudder and fuselage trim were medium blue. (R. O'Dell via Harry Gann) VA-66 A-4Cs, BuNos 148459 AF/301, 148463 AF/305, 148470 AF/304, and 148452 AF/303, assigned to the USS Intrepid (CVA-11) in 1962. (USN via Barry Miller)

the East Coast. VA-66's first A-4C Mediterranean deployment was made aboard Intrepid from 3 August 1961 to 1 March 1962 where they were honored as the top attack

squadron deployed with the Sixth Fleet. In February 1962, CO, CDR Jack Herman, placed first in the CAG-6 bombing derby with LTJG Paul Smoot placing second in the over all Top Gun competition.

On 25 May 1962, LT Raymond W. Hill in BuNo 149534 blew a tire on takeoff, swerved off the runway and caught fire at Patrick AFB. Then, from 3 August to 11 October 1962, VA-64 deployed to the Med aboard the USS Enterprise (CVAN-65). On 14 August 1962, the squadron participated in cross-

Above, VA-66 A-4C, BuNo 145099 AF/504, assigned to the USS Enterprise (CVAN-65) refuels a VF-102 F4H-1 on 20 August 1962. (USN) Below, VA-66 A-4C, BuNo 148459 AF/301, from CVA-11 while armed with two Bullpups in 1962. (USN via Barry Miller) Bottom, VA-66 A-4C, BuNo 148452 AF/303, taxis after trapping aboard the USS Intrepid (CVA-11) in 1962. (USN)

Above, VA-66 A-4C, BuNo 148452 AF/503, refuels VAH-7 A-5A while CAG bird A-4C, BuNo 148455 AF/00, waits it turn on 20 August 1962. (USN) At right, VA-66 A-4C, BuNo 148466 AF/511, on the hangar deck of CVAN-65 in 1962. (USN) Below right, VA-66 A-4C, BuNo 149543 AE/300, assigned to the USS America (CVA-66) In 1965. (Ginter collection) Bottom, manned VA-66 A-4Cs aboard the USS America (CVA-66) in 1967. BuNos 148459 AE/301, 149530 AE/314, 147830 AE/316, 147789 AE/306, and 148543 AE/511. (USN)

deck operations with the British carrier HMS Hermes. From aboard Enterprise, the squadron participated in the Cuban Blockade in October. On 26 October 1962, CDR Kent L. Lee ejected safely at sea from BuNo 149443.

A second CVAN-65 deployment

to the Med was made from 6 February to 4 September 1963.

A third CVAN-65 deployment, a world cruise, was conducted from 8 February to 3 October 1964. The ship operated near Cyprus in March 1964 to keep tabs on a conflict between Turkish and Greek Cypriots, after which Operation Sea Orbit, the first circumnavigation of the world by a nuclear task force, commenced.

From 30 October 1965 to 10 August 1966, VA-66 deployed aboard the USS America (CVA-66). During the cruise, LTJG Seldon M. Small ejected safely at sea from BuNo 149634 on 2 June 1966.

Another CVA-66 deployment was made from 10 January to 20 September 1967. On 4 March 1967 LTJG William H. Lifsey and LCDR J.D. Rasmussen in BuNos 147848

and 149543 collided in mid-air and ejected safely. LTJG Lifsey received a broken arm. Later that month, on 25 May, LCDR A.P. Lowry ejected safely from BuNo 147811 shortly after takeoff from CVA-66. On 8 June 1967, VA-66's aircraft were part of a CAW-6 strike group that was launched to defend the USS Liberty (AGTR-5) from the accidental attack by the Israelis.

1968 found VA-66 reassigned to CVW-10 where they deployed to Vietnam aboard the USS Intrepid (CVS-11) from 4 June 1968 to 8 February 1969. On 1 August 1968, the squadron lost LTJG E.J. Broms, Jr. in BuNo 148599 AK/301 to AAA over Dong Dun.

During training on 16 June 1969, LTJG Paul Fontaine ejected safely from BuNo 149601, which crashed and burned. The squadron's last A-

Above, VA-66 A-4C, BuNo 145122 AK/301, at Long Beach on 18 February 1969. Blue bomb below the canopy had 91 written on it for the number of bombing missions it flew in Vietnam. (Clay Jansson) Bottom, VA-66 A-4C, BuNo 149587 AK/306, on 18 February 1969. Blue bomb below the canopy had 80 written on it for the number of bombing missions it flew. (H. Gann)

4C deployment was with CVW-17 aboard the USS Forrestal (CVA-59) from 2 December 1969 through 8 July 1970. On 6 May 1970, BuNo 149524 AA/302, crashed into the water on take-off. LCDR J.E. Morrison was recovered by helicopter without injuries. In June 1970, the Popular Front for the Liberation of Palestine took hostages in Amman, Jordan, causing the Forrestal to move its operations off shore until the incident was resolved.

ATTACK SQUADRON SEVENTY - TWO, VA-72 "BLUE HAWKS"

Attack Squadron Seventy-Two (VA-72) was established as Fighter Bomber Squadron Eighteen (VBF-18) on 25 January 1945. VBF-18 was originally equipped with F6F-3/5 Hellcats. On 10 August 1945, they re-equipped with F8F-1s and took on the nickname Bearcats. VBF-18 was redesignated VF-8A on 15 November 1946. Then on 28 July 1948, VF-8A became VF-72. In 1950, the squadron adopted the nickname Hawks. The squadron flew F8F-1s/1Bs and F8F-2s before converting to Grumman F9F-2 Panthers on 16 March 1951. Then, on 3 January 1956, they became Attack Squadron Seventy-Two (VA-72). The squadron was flying F9F-5s when they transitioned to A4D-1 Skyhawks in September 1956. On 12 February 1958, the squadron traded-in their A4D-1s for A4D-2s. These, in turn, were replaced with A4D-2Ns in March 1961. The A-4E took over in May 1964, but the squadron reverted back to A-4Bs in March 1967. In January

1970, VA-72 transitioned to Vought A-7B aircraft. These were replaced with A-7Es in September 1977 and the squadron was disestablished on 30 June 1991.

VA-72 made three deployments to the Mediterranean aboard the USS Independence (CVA-62). The first was from 4 August to 19 December 1961. On 16 August, LCDR James A. Mulligan ejected safely from A4D-2N, BuNo 148461, when he lost his instruments at night and rolled inverted on final.

The second Mediterranean deployment of (CVA-62) was from 19 April to 27 August 1962.

From 22 October to 22 November 1962, during the Bay of Pigs invasion, CVA-62 and VA-72 operated south of Guantanamo Bay, Cuba.

From 10 through 16 May 1963, the squadron provided a three-plane

Above, VA-72 A4D-2N, BuNo 147845 AG/308, being re-spotted on CVA-62 in July 1961. (USN) Bottom, VA-72 A4D-2Ns, BuNos 148478 AG/303, 148479 AG/304, 147847 AG/308, and 147837 AG/310, in flight in 1961. Note stylized hawk head on the side of the fuselage. (USN)

Det for courier service from the USS Wasp (CVS-18) during the Project Mercury space flight of the Faith 7 capsule.

The third Mediterranean deployment of CVA-62 was from 6 August 1963 to 4 March 1964. On 19 August, a flight of four Skyhawks got into trouble in bad weather. They could not land on CVA-62 or the divert field at Lann Bihoue at Lorient due to the weather. LTJG Herbert Recktenwald in BuNo 148579 AG/305 and LTJG Duane Tut in BuNo 149512 AG/301 both ejected when they ran out of fuel. A VA-86 pilot in BuNo 149631

AG/407 also ran out of fuel and ejected. The 4th plane landed in France. Four days later, LT Steven Kadas in BuNo 148568, collided with the round-down ramp while landing at night. The plane disintegrated and went into the water. LT Kadas was never recovered.

Above, VA-72 A4D-2N, BuNo 147845 AG/308, being re-spotted from the elevator to the hangar deck on CVA-62 in July 1961. (USN) Below, A-4Cs, BuNos 147845 AG/312, 148479 AG/304, and 149512 AG/301, over CVA-62 in 1963. (USN)

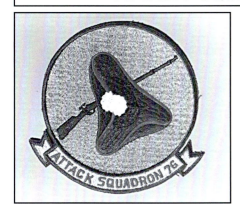

Attack Squadron Seventy-Six (VA-76) was established on 1 June 1955 at NAS Oceana, VA, with the primary mission of atomic weapons delivery. The F2H-2 Banshee was flown until 6 January 1956 when the first F9F-8 Cougar arrived. On 28 May 1959, the first A4D-2 Skyhawk was delivered to VA-76. On 30 June 1959, CDR Cheuvronr delivered the last fleet F9F-8 to the Reserve Command. The A-4C arrived on 2 March 1962 and the squadron was disestablished on 30 September 1969.

Seven deployments were made with the A4D-2N/A-4C by VA-76. The first five of these were aboard the USS Enterprise (CVAN-65), the first one being the "Big E's" shakedown from 3 August to 11 October 1962 to the Mediterranean as part of CVG-6. During this cruise, President John F. Kennedy visited the ship and on 9 August the Air Group conducted cross-deck exercises with the Royal

Above, a VA-76 line member installs (Zaps) a squadron patch on a Royal Navy Sea Vixen during cross-deck operations on 9 August 1962. (USN) VA-76 A-4Cs on the forward deck of the USS Enterprise (CVAN-65) on 2 July 1962. At the left of the photo is BuNo 149522 AF/606 and 149529 AF/611. Note Crusader landing in background. (USN)

Above, VA-76 A-4C, BuNo 147704 AE/501, on the elevator of CVAN-65 in 1964. (USN) Below, VA-76 A-4C, BuNo 149630 AE/605, launching from CVAN-65 in 1964 with practice bombs. (USN)

Navy during Exercise Riptide III.

The second CVAN-65 cruise was to the Caribbean in response to the Cuban Missile Crisis and naval block-ade aboard the "Big E" from 19 October to 3 December 1962.

Another Enterprise deployment to the Med was conducted from 6 February to 4 September 1963.

On 2 February 1964, LT J,W. Thornton was killed when BuNo 148455 crashed in the ocean shortly after takeoff from NAS Oceana on a night training flight.

From 8 February to 3 October 1964, the squadron participated in Operation Sea Orbit, a world cruise aboard CVAN-65. Ports of call were: Crete, Istanbul, Cannes, Naples, Genova, Les Salin, Palermo, Taranto, Barcelona, Palma, Pollensa Bay, Rabat, Dakar, Freetown, Monrovia, Abidjan, Nairobi, Karachi, Freemantle, Melbourne, Sydney, Wellington, Buenos Aires, Montevideo, Sao Paulo, Rio De

Janeiro, Recife, and Norfolk. In March, the squadron operated near Cyprus the during Turk-Greek Cypriot crisis.

A crisis in the Dominican Republic had VA-76 shore based at Naval Station Roosevelt Roads, PR, from where they flew armed reconnaissance flights from 29 May to 15 June 1965. CVW-6 was working up for the shakedown cruise of the new USS America (CVA-66) scheduled for November 1965. VA-76's A-4Cs were initially painted up for this event until the squadron was reassigned to CVW-9 for CVAN-65's first war cruise as the size of the ship required an additional attack squadron be embarked.

The last Enterprise deployment was a war cruise to Vietnam from 26 October 1965 to 21 June 1966 as part of CVW-9. On 22 December 1965, LT J.D. Prudhomme was killed-in-action

Above, VA-76 A-4C, BuNo 148485 AE/505, in short-lived CVA-66 markings in July 1965. Rudder and drop tank trim was green. (R. Esposito via Norm Taylor) Bottom, VA-76 A-4C, BuNo 147704 AE/501, was the first fixed wing aircraft loaded aboard the USS America for its first carrier trials. It then became the first aircraft to take off and land aboard CVA-66. For this event, CDR Kenneth B. Austin, the ship's Executive Officer, flew 147704 on 5 April 1965. (USN)

Above, VA-76 A-4C, tanking a RVAH-7 RA-5C off Vietnam in 1966. (USN K31296) At left, bombed-up VA-76 A-4C, BuNo 147792 NG/510, launches on a mission to Vietnam in 1966. (USN) Bottom, bombed-up VA-72 A-4C, BuNo 148485 NG/505, being spotted on the USS Enterprise (CVAN-65) in 1966. (USN)

by AAA over the North in BuNo 149521 NG/502. VA-76 lost a second pilot on 2 January 1966 when LTJG D.C. MacLaughlin was downed by AAA over the South in BuNo 147704 NG/501. A third A-4C, BuNo 148444 NG/502, was lost to enemy action on 25 March 1966. The enemy's AAA had made LTJG B.E. Smith become a POW. During the cruise, the

squadron accumulated 2,147 combat sorties, 5,124 flight hours, 2,548 carrier landings and dropped 3,367,257 pounds of ordnance on enemy targets.

On 29 October 1966, LT Charles Nelson died on a training flight out of NAS Fallon, NV, in BuNo 149960.

One month prior to their second war deployment, on 6 December 1966, CO, CDR Albert D. McFall, was lost following a night catapult launch from CVA-31 in BuNo 149549. For VA-76's sixth A-4C deployment, the squadron joined CVW-21 aboard the USS Bon Homme Richard (CVA-31) for another Vietnam War cruise from 26 January to 25 August 1967.

On 1 May 1967, history was made when LCDR Ted R. Swartz became the one-and-only A-4 pilot to shoot down a MiG-17 in BuNo 148609 NP/685. Swartz had just fired several Zuni rockets at two MiG-17s on Kep airfield when he got a radio call of two MiGs on his tail. He put his A-4C into a high barrel roll and got behind the MiGs, then fired his last Zunis downing one of the MiGs. On this cruise, CVA-31's F-8 Crusaders downed an additional eight MiG-17s.

Above, VA-76 A-4C, BuNo 147799 NP/333, on 10 September 1966 with the CVW-21 NP tail code applied. (Duane Kasulka) Below, VA-76 A-4C, BuNo 149540 NP/690, landing at Atsugi in 1967. (Ginter collection) Bottom, VA-76 A-4C, BuNo 148314 NP/681, at NAS Alameda, CA, assigned to the USS Bon Homme Richard on 25 September 1967. Fin tip and rudder were black. (Harry Gann)

NOON raid
MAY-1-1967   VA 76 Side #. 685   BuNo 148609
USS Bon Homme Richard Air Wing 21
                                                    8-10000'
Clear (hazy) day- some - about 3/10 - 2/10 medium
    cumulus -

Mission   Airwing strike on kep airfield -
- Flak suppress
- Engaged MIG after left roll in and run + left
    turn - HiG roll put MIG 500-700' out in front
- shot zuni - missed - shot another - VT fuze
    hit, port wing root of left MIG

A/c was configured with c/L (400) and 4 LAU 10
    zuni pods

Altitude 2500' just NorthEast of runway at KEA
    port turn - 2 MIGs in close section formation
    standard green brown camouflage - red star
    10° look down angle on shot -
    MIGs in 60° bank left
    A4 in 45° bank left

            Cdr TR Swartz VF 121
                NAS Miramar 92042

On the negative side, four VA-76 Skyhawks were downed to enemy action. The first was BuNo 147799 NP/603 on 25 April 1967. LCDR C.D. Stackhouse became a POW after being downed by a MiG. AAA got BuNo 147816 NP/683, piloted by XO CDR K.R. Cameron, on 18 May 1967. CDR Cameron died in captivity. Two pilots were downed on 14 July 1967 over the North. CO CDR R.B. Fuller became a POW after being hit with a SAM in BuNo 147709 NP/688 and LT J.W. Donis was recovered after being downed by AAA in BuNo 147759 NP/693.

The squadron's last A-4C deployment was to the Med with CVW-7 aboard the USS Independence (CVA-62) from 30 April 1968 to 27 January 1969. During the cruise, on 21 December, LCDR R.M. Mulrooney failed to return from a flight in BuNo 147683 AG/306.

At left, MiG-17 shoot-down recap by CDR T.R. Swartz written on back of a NAS Miramar Officer Mess placemat in 1975. (Harry Gann) Below left, VA-76 A-4C assigned to CDR Joe Barth, BuNo 149645 AG/301, while assigned to the USS Independence (CVA-62) on 15 February 1969. It appears that all squadron aircraft had Swartz's MiG-17 applied to the fuselage side just behind the intake. (Roy Lock via Nick Williams) Bottom, VA-76 A-4C, BuNo 147683 AG/306, assigned to LCDR Buddy Owens aboard the USS Independence (CVA-62) in 1968. Note red MiG-17 behind the intake. (Ginter collection)

Anti-Submarine Fighter Squadron Seventy-Six (VSF-76) was originally established on paper as VSF-IIX2 in July 1968. In 1970, it was split into VSF-75XI and VSF-70XI, then these units became VSF-76 as part of CVSGR-70. From 17 to 26 August 1971, the squadron conducted training operations from the USS Wasp (CVS-18).

VSF-76 was disestablished on 1 September 1973. Its assets, including those from VSF-86 and VF-753, were used to form Fleet Composite Squadron Thirteen (VC-13).

VSF-76 operated nine A-4Cs: BuNos 147714, 147797, 147830, 148491, 148591, 148593, 149530, 149537, and 149618. One A-4B, BuNo 145082 also was utilized.

Above, VSF-76 A-4C, BuNo 149618 AW/663, on 17 August 1971. Note hoisting bridle atop aircraft and USS Wasp painted next to it. (Joe Weathers) Below, VSF-76 A-4C, BuNo 149618 AW/603, in 1971. Rudder and fin tip were black. (Joe Weathers collection) Bottom, VSF-76 A-4C CAG bird, BuNo 149530 AW/660, on 20 July 1971. Fin tip and drop tank trim were black and rudder was red, yellow, blue, orange, green, black. (Craig Kaston collection)

ATTACK SQUADRON EIGHTY-ONE, VA-81 "SUNLINERS"

VA-81 originally was established as VA-66 on 1 July 1955 and redesignated that same day as Fighter Squadron Eighty-One. The Crusaders of VF-81 were assigned the mission of special weapons delivery in their Grumman F9F-8 and F9F-8B Cougars. On 4 March 1959, VF-81 was re-equipped with A4D-2 Skyhawks and on 1 July 1959, VF-81 was redesignated Attack Squadron Eighty-One.

The squadron received A-4Es on 3 April 1963 and was renamed the Sunliners. Three A-4E deployments were made with the last one ending on 20 May 1967. They then re-equipped with A-4Cs as the more advanced Echos were needed as

replacements for those lost in combat. The squadron's first A-4C was received on 1 June 1967.

The squadron made two Mediterranean deployments with the A-4C. The first was from 15 November 1967 through 4 August

Above, squadron CO, CDR M.D. Cunningham, during VA-81's CVA-38 deployment in 1968, prepares for a mission. (USN) Below, BuNos 147829 AJ/401, 145076 AJ/403, 149531 AJ/412, and 149646 AJ/410, over the USS Shangri La (CVA-38) in 1967 while on cruise in the Mediterranean. Tail trim was orange. (USN)

Above, VA-81 A-4C, BuNo 147748 AB/401, from CVA-67 with VF-14 Phantoms in 1969. (USN via Tailhhok) Below, VA-81 A-4C, BuNo 149500 AB/402, traps aboard the USS John F. Kennedy on 21 October 1968. (USN via Tailhhok) Bottom, VA-81 A-4C, BuNo 147748 AB/401, being prepped on the JFK in 1968. Tail markings were orange. (USN)

1968 aboard the USS Shangri-La (CVA-38) as part of CVW-8.

The second A-4C deployment was from 5 April through 21 December 1969 aboard the USS John F. Kennedy (CVA-67) as part of CVW-1. This was JFK's first deployment. The squadron operated off the coast of Libya following a 1 September coup that overthrew Libya's monarchy. Following the deployment, in February 1970, VA-81 was awarded the Navy Battle "E" for the best East Coast A-4 squadron.

The A-4Cs were replaced with A-7E Corsair II aircraft in May 1970. These were replaced with F/A-18Cs on 30 March 1988 and VA-81 became Fighter Attack Squadron Eighty-One (VFA-81).

Below, VA-81 A-4Cs, BuNos 149531 AB/400, 147814 AB/412, 147748 AB/401 and 149502 AB/415, on the JFK in 1968. (USN via Tailhhok)

Above, VA-81 A-4C, BuNo 147717 AB/404, with orange tail trim in 1968. (Clay Jansson) Below, VA-81 A-4C ordered to launch from the JFK in 1968. (USN via Mark Aldrich)

ATTACK SQUADRON EIGHTY - THREE, VA-83 "RAMPAGERS"

The origins of VA-83 can be traced back to Fighter Squadron Nine Hundred Sixteen. VF-916, a reserve squadron, was called to active duty on 1 February 1951 while at NAS Squantum, MA, with F4U-4 Corsairs. The squadron moved to NAS Jacksonville, FL, with the Grumman F9F-2 Panther. In September 1951, VF-916 was transferred to NAS Oceana, VA, prior to receiving

Grumman F8F-2 Bearcats in May 1952. In September, the Bearcats gave way to F9F-5 Panthers. In February 1953, VF-916 was redesignated Fighter Squadron Eighty-Three. The Vought F7U-3 became the next aircraft for VF-83 in May 1954. In February 1956, VF-83 was redesignated Attack Squadron Eighty-Three while flying F7U-3Ms. In March 1957, VA-83 began transition-

Above, VA-83 A4D-2N, BuNo 147811 AJ/301, assigned to the CO CDR Bud Nance in France on 10 June 1961. (USN) Below, VA-83 AD-4Ns, BuNos 147807 AJ/302, 147818 AJ/314, 147801 AJ/306, and 147814 AJ/312, over the USS Forrestal (CVA-59) on 10 July 1961. (USN)

ing to the A4D-1 Skyhawk. The A4D-

Above, VA-83 A4D-2N, BuNo 147806 AJ/303, at the Paris Airshow in June 1961. (Ginter collection) Below, VA-83 A-4C, BuNo 147801 AJ/306, tanks a Royal Navy Scimitar from the HMS Hermes as a KA-3B prepares to tank a Royal Navy Sea Vixen while a VFP-62 RF-8A shadows the flight in August 1962. (USN C94371) Bottom, two VA-83 A-4Cs, BuNos 148546 AJ/308 and 150595 AJ/314, from the USS Shangri-La (CVA-38) over the Med in 1968. Rudder and drop tank trim were blue. (USN)

1s were replaced with A4D-2s in December 1957, which were in turn replaced with A4D-2Ns in September 1960. In May 1963, the squadron received A-4Es. Because of a depletion of A-4Es in combat in Vietnam, VA-83 was forced to give up its Echos as replacements for other squadrons. They then re-equipped with A-4Cs in August 1967. Vought A-7Es replaced the Skyhawks on 19 June 1970. The squadron was redesignated Fighter Attack Squadron Eighty-Three on 25 April 1988 when it received the F/A-18C.

The squadron's first A4D-2N (A-4C) deployment was aboard the USS Forrestal (CVA-59) to the Mediterranean from 9 February through 25 August 1961 as part of CVG-8. During this cruise, VA-83 aircraft participated in the Paris Air Show.

A second A-4C deployment to the Med was made by VA-83 aboard CVA-59 from 3 August 1962 through 2 March 1963. The squadron cross-decked with the British carrier HMS Hermes in August 1962 while on the way to the Med. On 7 February 1963, LTJG Warren J. Blanke Jr. was killed in BuNo 147805 during a bombing dive astern of the ship.

A third CVW-8 A-4C deployment to the Med was made aboard the USS Shangri-La (CVA-38) from 15

Above, VA-83 JFK pilots and officers. kneeling left-to-right: S.D. Wilson, R.E. Fisher, R.L. Kjosa, T.C. Casimes, F.J. Almberg, J.D. Wolff, J.T. Petillo, M.B.C. Wiles, T.J. Giardina, P.H. Coussens. Standing left-to-right: L.E. Garrett, J.S. McKee, J.J. Brabenec, J.P. Richman, D.B. Caldwell, M.J. Concannon, R.A. Bohlman, R.J. Van Ort, E.M. Duben, S.J. Wegert, W.E. Newman, C.P. McCullough, R.P. Bush, F.R. Wesh, and W.B. McLaird. (USN) Bottom, VA-83 A-4C, BuNo 147726 AB/303, over the USS John F. Kennedy (CVA-67) in September 1969 while armed with Zuni rockets. (USN)

November 1967 through 4 August 1968.

The fourth and last A-4C deployment by VA-83 was aboard the USS John F. Kennedy (CVA-67) from 5 April through 21 December 1969. During the month of September 1969,

the squadron and ship were ordered to operate off the coast of Libya following a coup that overthrew the Libyan monarchy on 1 September 1969. On 19 October 1969, LCDR John D. Wolff was killed when he crashed BuNo 148546 AJ/300 into a mountain side.

ATTACK SQUADRON EIGHTY - SIX, VA-86 "SIDEWINDERS"

On 1 February 1951, reserve Fighter Squadron VF-921 was called to active duty in response to the Korean War. The squadron flew the F4U-4, F8F-2 and F9F-5 before being redesignated VF-84 on 4 February 1953. On 1 July 1955, the squadron was redesignated Attack Squadron Eighty-Six. As VA-86 they flew the F7U-3M until 26 May 1957, when they were replaced with the A4D-1 Skyhawk. In December 1957, the A4D-2 was acquired and in September 1962 the A-4C was received. These were replaced with A-4Es on 28 April 1964. In February 1967, the squadron transitioned to the Vought A-7A Corsair II. On 8 February 1989, VA-86 was redesignated VFA-86 and transitioned to the F/A-18C Hornet.

In November 1962, the squadron operated from the USS Lexington (CVS-16) off the coast of Jacksonville, FL, in an on-call condition during the Cuban Missile Crisis. Then, in April through May 1963, the squadron provided Sidewinder equipped detachments aboard the carriers USS Randolph (CVS-15), USS Essex (CVS-9) and the USS Wasp (CVS-18)

The squadron made only one A-4C deployment from 6 August 1963 through 4 March 1964 aboard the USS Independence (CVA-62) as part of CVG-7. The cruise was to the Mediterranean and the Atlantic. During the cruise, LT W.R. Hall lost BuNo 149631 AG/407 when he ran out of fuel over the water off the coast of France in heavy weather. Two other A-4Cs from VA-72 in the same flight were lost over the coast of France, also due to fuel starvation.

Below, VA-86 A-4C, BuNo 149636 AG/409, aboard the USS Independence (CVA-62) in 1963. (USN via A. Romano) Bottom, VA-86 A-4C, BuNo 149638 AG/409, at McGuire AFB. Trim including snakes head was orange. Tail code "AG" was boardered by orange, too. (Frank MacSorley)

NFO TRAINING SQUADRON EIGHTY - SIX,   VT-86 "SABERHAWKS"

VT-86 was established on 5 June 1972 at NAS Glynco, GA, under the command of CDR George C. Eckerd and originally was part of Training Air Wing Eight. The squadron's main mission was to provide advanced Naval Flight Officer (NFO) training. The training was in four areas: Radar Intercept Operations (RIOs), Advanced Jet Navigation (AJN), Airborne Electronic Warfare and Airborne Tactical Data Systems.

Initially, it used aircraft on loan from NATTC before acquiring its own aircraft in February 1973. These were two A-4Bs, BuNos 145097 and 145100; eighteen A-4Cs, 147691, 147701, 147726, 147731, 147797, 147838, 147841, 148304, 148469, 148482, 148493, 148526, 148558, 148576, 148605, 149530, 149537, and 149563; twenty-four T-39Ds; two EC-121Ks; and twelve TS-2As. After receiving these aircraft on 28 February 1973, the squadron's mission was expanded to include flight support for Air Intercept Control and Ground Controlled Approach training functions.

On 28 February 1974, a VT-86 detachment was established at NAS Pensacola, FL, following a decision to close NAS Glynco and disestablish TRAWING-8 as part of the post-Vietnam budget cuts. VT-86 transfered to TRAWING-6 at Pensacola on 1 June 1974. With the move, the squadron's A-4Cs, EC-121Ks and TS-2As were retired from service. The TA-4J was acquired on 21 May 1974 and by the end of the year the squadron had eleven TA-4Js, and twenty T-39Ds.

VT-86 A-4C, BuNo 148526 4B/20, at NAS Glynco, GA, on 8 October 1973. Trim on the nose, sword, drop tank, and tail were yellow highlighted by black. (Fred Roos) Bottom, VT-86 A-4C, BuNo 145097 4B/18, on 8 October 1973. (Fred Roos)

ANTI - SUBMARINE FIGHTER SQUADRON EIGHTY - SIX, VSF-86 "GATORS"

VSF-86 was the second New Orleans-based anti-submarine fighter squadron (see VSF-76). VSF-86 was assigned to CVSGR-80 and was established as VSF-11X2 in July 1968 with a few A-4Bs. The squadron then was split into VSF-80X3 and VSF-85X4 which became VSF-86 in 1970 with the re-organization of the reserves. Eight A-4Cs were acquired begining on 3 June 1970. These were BuNos 148304, 148463, 148464, 148517, 148589, 149563, 149581, and 149635. The A-4Cs were replaced by F-8Hs in late 1971 and VSF-76 and VSF-86 were combined and redesignated VC-13 in August 1973.

VSF-86 deployed aboard the USS Ticonderoga (CVS-14) from July through August 1971, during which CDR Etheridge relieved CDR Kloves as CO on 15 August.

Below, VSF-86 A-4C, BuNo 148463 NW/601, in 1971. (USN via Joe Weathers) Bottom, VSF-86 A-4C, BuNo 148463, aboard the USS Ticonderoga (CVA-18) in August 1971. (USN)

ATTACK SQUADRON NINETY - THREE, VA-93 "BLUE BLAZERS"

Below, VA-93 A-4Cs aboard the USS Ranger (CVA-61) as it passes through the Heyano Seato Straits while enroute to Iwakuni, Japan, on 5 April 1963. BuNo 149523 NG/312 is in the foreground. (USN)

VA-93 originally was established as Fighter Squadron Ninety-Three (VF-93) on 26 March 1952. VF-93 initially was equipped with FG-1D Corsairs and F9F-2 Panthers in September 1953 and then with F9F-8 Cougars in January 1955. On 15 September 1956, VF-93 was redesignated Attack Squadron Ninety-Three (VA-93) and on 26 November 1956 received the A4D-1 Skyhawk. The A4D-2 replaced the -1s on 25 May 1958 and in turn were replaced with A4D-2N on 1 September 1960. The squadron's A-4Cs were replaced by A-4Es in September 1966 and A-4Fs were acquired in September 1967. These were traded in for the Vought A-7B on 20 April 1969. The squadron then flew various versions of the Corsair II's until 31 August 1986 when the unit was disestablished.

VA-93's first A4D-2N deployment was from 11 August 1961 through 8 March 1962 aboard the USS Ranger (CVA-61) as part of CVG-9. During this Westpac cruise, on 17 August 1961, BuNo 147700 was damaged beyond repair in a deck accident and was stricken.

From 9 November 1962 through 14 June 1963, A-4Cs went aboard CVA-61 again as part of CVG-9. The squadron received the 1962 Battle Efficiency "E" as the outstanding West Coast light jet attack squadron. In May 1963, the Ranger arrived off Laos and Vietnam to support possible operations in Laos following Laotion losses to the Pathet Lao in the Plaine de Jarres.

VA-93's Det Q with A-4Bs, first received in 15 October 1963, was aboard the USS Bennington (CVS-20) from 19 February through 11 September 1964 as part of CVSG-59.

From 5 August 1964 through 6 May 1965, VA-93 flew from the USS Ranger (CVA-61) on the squadron's first Vietnam War cruise. No aircraft were lost to any cause and the squadron won the Chief of Naval Operations Safety Award in 1965. On 7 February 1965, VA-93 participated in Flaming Dart I, a reprisal strike against the military barracks at Vit Thu Lu which was aborted due to weather. Four days later, another strike, Flaming Dart II, was successful against the barracks at Chanh Hoa, North Vietnam. On 15 March, the squadron attacked the ammunition storage sites in Phu Qui, North Vietnam during Rolling Thunder strikes.

Above, VA-93 A-4C, BuNo 147720 NG/305, assigned to CVA-61. (Ginter collection) Bottom, VA-93 A-4C, BuNo 149508 NG/303, being prepped for launch from the USS Ranger while off the coast of Vietnam on 24 March 1965. Note small practice bombs on the wing racks. (USN)

The squadron's last A-4C deployment was a war cruise aboard the USS Enterprise (CVAN-65) from 16 October 1965 through 21 June 1966 as part of CVW-9. On 2 December 1965, VA-93 flew the first combat mission ever launched from a nuclear-powered carrier. Commonly known as the Blue Blazers, VA-93 earned the nickname of Bridge Busters in May 1966 when the squadron pilots downed seven important highway and railroad bridges in two days. Although no combat losses occurred during the deployment, LCDR John B. Tapp was killed when

he flew into the water 10 miles astern of the ship during an instrument approach in BuNo 147738 NG/302. During the cruise, VA-93 pilots flew 2,247 combat sorties and dropped three million pounds of ordnance on enemy targets.

Above, VA-93 A-4C, BuNo 147710 NG/310, at NAS Lemoore on 10 September 1966 with bomb mission marks on the rear fuselage. Drop tanks were black, rudder trim was blue, and stylized planes were blue and black with red exhaust trails. (Duane Kasulka) At right, bombed-up VA-93 A-4C, BuNo 149505 NG/316, on CVAN-65's cat in 1966. (USN) Below, VA-93 A-4Cs, BuNos 147720 NG/305, NG/310, 149505 NG/316, and NG/301, enroute to a target in 1966. (USN)

ATTACK SQUADRON NINETY - FOUR, VA-94 "SHRIKES"

Fighter Squadron Ninety-Four (VF-94) was established on 26 March 1952. VF-94 flew F4U Corsairs, FJ-3 Furies, and F8F-8B Cougars before being redesignated Attack Squadron Ninety-Four on 1 August 1958. As VA-94, the squadron transitioned to the FJ-4B Fury. In January 1959,

A4D-2s replaced the Fury Bravos. In September 1960, A4D-2Ns were acquired to replace the A4D-2s. On 23 October 1967, the A-4E replaced the squadron's A-4Cs and on 16 November they received their first "Super Echo". The squadron transitioned to the Vought A-7E Corsair II in January 1971. The Corsair IIs were replaced with F/A-18C Hornets in May 1990 and the squadron was redesignated VFA-94 on 28 June 1990.

The squadron's first A4D-2N/A-4C deployment was aboard the USS Ranger (CVA-61) from 11 August 1961 through 8 March 1962 as part of a CVG-9 WestPac cruise.

A second Western Pacific deployment was made aboard CVA-61 from

9 November 1962 through 14 June 1963.

While in training at NAS Lemoore, CA, on 6 March 1964, LT Thomas E. Dunlap safely ejected from BuNo 147730 8 miles west of Tulare.

VA-94's third A-4C cruise was a combat deployment aboard CVA-61

Below, the old and the new. VA-94 A4D-2N. BuNo 147719 NG/402, poses with a VA-95 Skyraider in September 1960. A stylized orange Shrike was applied to the drop tanks. (USN) Bottom, 147719 later in its career aboard the USS Ranger (CVA-61). The improved version of the nose cone has been installed and the orange Shrike has been moved to the fuselage. (USN)

from 5 August 1964 through 6 May 1965. The squadron participated in Yankee Team Operations and Flaming Dart I and II and in Rolling Thunder strikes. No aircraft were lost during this cruise.

A second Vietnam War cruise was conducted aboard the USS Enterprise (CVAN-65) from 26 October 1965 through 21 June 1966 as part of CVW-9. On 23 December 1965, LTJG W.L. Shankel became a POW after his A-4C, BuNo 149562 NG/414, was shot down by AAA over the North. LTJG F.C. Baldock, Jr., also became a POW when BuNo 147740 NG/401 was downed by a SAM on 17 March 1966. Four days later, LT F.R. Compton in BuNo 149515 NG/406 and LCDR J.M. Tiderman in 148499 NG/411 were killed-in-action by a SAM off the coast of North Vietnam. During the cruise, VA-94

Above, VA-94 A-4C, BuNo 147740 NG/408, with small Shrike on tail and a large one on the drop tank. (Clay Jansson) Below, four VA-94 A-4Cs returning from a strike over Vietnam while assigned to the USS Ranger (CVA-61) in 1964. BuNos 147737 NG/406, 147742 NG/409, 147735 NG/404 and 149577 NG/407. (USN)

Above, four VA-94 A-4Cs over the USS Ranger (CVA-61) in 1964. (USN) Below, four VA-94 A-4Cs, BuNos 149580 NG/400 (CAG bird), 147736 NG/405, 147740 NG/401 (CO's bird), and 147719 NG/402, on the deck of Ranger on 24 March 1965 with Hancock in the background. (USN)

Above, VA-94 A-4Cs, BuNos 149531 NG/412 and 149541 NG/413, aboard CVAN-65 in 1965. (USN) Below, VA-94 A-4C, BuNo 149515 NG/411, assigned to CVAN-65. (Harry Gann) Bottom, VA-94 A-4C, BuNo 149531 NG/412, assigned to the USS Enterprise (CVAN-65) while at NAS Lemoore, CA, on 21 August 1965. Fin tip and fuselage Shrike design were orange. (William Swisher)

flew 2,575 sorties and 4,952.3 flight hours.

While preparing for a Hancock deployment, LCDR Paul Barrish in BuNo 148308 collided with LTJG Robert Gordon from VF-53 in F-8E BuNo 150676 over the Chocolate Mountains on 7 October 1966. LCDR Barrish ejected safely while LTJG Gordon was killed.

The squadron's last A-4C deployment was aboard the USS Hancock (CVA-19) to Vietnam from 5 January to 22 July 1967 as part of CVW-5. On 30 March 1967, LT Richard J. Miles ejected safely alongside the ship when he ran out of fuel in BuNo 147844. CDR Roger M. Netherland was killed by a SAM-2 near Kien airfield 10 miles south of Haiphong in BuNo 149509 NF/404 on 10 May 1967.

VA-94 A-4C, 149538 NF/414, on CVA-19 on 31 May 1967. (USN) Below, VA-94 A-4C, BuNo 147839 NF/407, at NAS Alameda, CA, in November 1967. (S. Kraus via Norm Taylor) Bottom, VA-94 A-4C, BuNo 147681 NF/401, while assigned to the USS Hancock (CVA-19) on 12 September 1966. Note mission marks behind the Shrike's wing. (Harry Gann)

ATTACK SQUADRON NINETY - FIVE, VA-95 "GREEN LIZARDS"

Above, VA-95 A-4C, BuNo 147816 NG/501, in 1966. Fin tip, lizard, and drop tank trim were green. (Harry Gann) Below, VA-95 A-4C, BuNo 149508 AB/500, assigned to the USS John F. Kennedy (CVA-67) at NAS Alameda, CA, on 2 January 1969. Lizard and lance were black. (William Swisher) Bottom, VA-95 A-4C, BuNo 150586 AB/501, in 1969. (USN)

Attack Squadron Ninety-Five (VA-95) was established on 26 April 1952. Initially equipped with F6F-5 Hellcats, the squadron transitioned to AD Skyraiders in May and continued to employ various versions of the aircraft until 15 July 1965 when A-4C Skyhawks were received. A-4Bs replaced the A-4Cs in December 1965 and VA-95 became one of the few squadrons to deploy the Bravo model to the waters off Vietnam. The squadron made two cruises with the A-4Bs before returning to A-4Cs in September 1968. The squadron was disestablished on 1 April 1970.

VA-95 only made one deploy-ment with the A-4C. It was aboard the USS John F. Kennedy (CVA-67) from 5 April to 21 December 1969 as part of CVW-1. On 14 June, LT Robert E. Turgeon, Jr., ejected safely from his A-4C, BuNo 147739, into the bay of Naples during a firepower demonstration.

ATTACK SQUADRON ONE - ZERO - SIX, VA-106 "GLADIATORS"

Bomber Fighter Squadron Seventeen (VBF-17) was established on 2 January 1945 and equipped with F6F-5 Hellcats. It was redesignated Fighter Squadron Six B (VF-6B) on 15 November 1946 with F4U-4 Corsairs. The squadron was redesignated VF-62 on 28 July 1948 after receiving F8F-2 Bearcats. They then flew F8F-1Bs and F2H-2 Banshees before being redesignated Attack

Squadron One Hundred Six (VA-106) on 1 July 1955 after receiving F9F-8B Cougars. On 4 June 1958, the squadron converted to A4D-2 Skyhawks which were replaced with A-4Cs on 18 December 1962. In November 1966, the A-4E took over

Above, VA-106 A-4C, BuNo 149522 AK/311 aboard CVA-38 on 12 August 1964. (USN) Below, VA-106 A-4C, BuNo 148546 AK/309, weapons display at NAS Oceana, VA, on 11 February 1964. Tail and fuselage trim were medium blue. (Nick Williams collection)

Above, VA-106 A-4C, BuNo 148503 AC/403, taxis at Bevelcom Airport, Belgium, on 25 June 1966. (W. Snel via Norm Taylor) At left, VA-106 A-4C, BuNo 150585 AC/409, aboard the USS Saratoga (CVA-60) in Pollensa Bay when CVA-59, in the background, relieved the Sara in 1966. (USN via Angelo Romano) Bottom, VA-106 A-4C, BuNo 150070 AA/321, aboard the USS Forrestal (CVA-59) in 1967. (Tailhook)

and on 7 November 1969, VA-106 was disestablished.

VA-106 completed three deployments with the A-4C, all to the Mediterranean. The first of these was aboard the USS Shangri-La (CVA-38) from 1 October 1963 through 23 May 1964 as part of CVW-10. While the squadron was working-up for the

cruise, two aircraft were lost. On 11 July 1963, BuNo 149517 was damaged beyond repair and was stricken. Then on 22 July 1963, LT George D. Stathers Jr., was not recovered after he crashed BuNo 148478 into the Atlantic while training off CVA-38. After the cruise was completed, they also received the Bullpup missile Top Shot award for 1964.

The second A-4C CVA-38 deployment was from 15 February to 20 September 1965.

The third A-4C deployment was aboard the USS Saratoga (CVA-60) from 11 March 1966 to 26 October 1966 as part of CVW-3.

On 1 February 1967, VA-106 was reassigned to CVW-17 with an "AA" tail code. This was followed by a return to CVW-10 "AK" on 10 January 1968 and then in March 1969 the squadron was assigned to the USS Independence (CVA-62) and CVW-17's "AG" tail code. However, no deployments were made with any of these Air Wings.

At right top-to-bottom: VA-106 A-4C, BuNo 149573 AG-313, on CVA-62 in 1969. (Ginter col.) VA-106 A-4C, BuNo 147768 AG-314, in 1969. (Ginter col.) VA-106 A-4C, BuNo 148612 AG/315, in 1969. (Ginter col.) Bottom, VA-106 A-4C, BuNo 148517 AG/310, in June 1969. Rudder and fuselage helmet were medium blue; fuselage arrow was yellow. (Duane Kasulka)

133

ATTACK SQUADRON ONE HUNDRED TWELVE, VA-112 "BRONCOS"

VA-112 started out as Fighter Bomber Squadron Eleven (VBF-11) on 17 August 1945 with the F6F Hellcat. In November 1946, VBF-11 was redesignated VF-12A and the squadron received F8F Bearcats in December 1946. VF-12A became VF-112 on 15 July 1948 with F9F

Panthers replacing the Bearcats on 11 January 1950. The squadron upgraded to the swept-wing Cougar in September 1953. Then, on 5 April 1957, the squadron equipped with the Sparrow missile-armed F3H-2M Demon. On 15 February 1959, VF-112 was redesignated Attack Squadron One Hundred Twelve (VA-112) and received the Douglas A4D-2 Skyhawk. The A4D-2Ns (A-4Cs) replaced the A4D-2s on 26 March 1961. VA-112 was disestablished on 10 October 1969.

On 22 July 1961, during a night training flight from NAS Miramar, CA, to NAS South Weymouth, MA, BuNo 147849 was lost in a mid-air. LTJG Donald K. Law ejected safely after colliding with LT David F. Callahan near Memphis. LT Callahan landed

his badly damaged jet safely at Millington. Then, on 11 September 1961, VA-112 moved from Miramar to NAS Lemoore, CA.

The first of six A-4C deployments was a WestPac cruise aboard the USS Kitty Hawk (CVA-63) from 13 September 1962 through 2 April 1963 as part of CVG-11.

Another WestPac deployment was made aboard CVA-63 from 17 October 1963 through 20 July 1964

Below, four VA-112 A-4Cs, BuNos 145127 NH/213, 148442 NH/204, 148449 NH/207 and 148447 NH/201, 3,000 feet over Mono Lake, CA, on 4 April 1962. Fin tips were yellow over a thin black line. (USN)

Above, VA-112 A-4C, BuNo 147714 AJ/504, assigned to the USS Forrestal (CVA-59) in 1964. Fin tip remained yellow. (Harry Gann) At right, VA-112 A-4C, BuNo 147721 NH/401 after trapping aboard the Kitty Hawk in 1965. Fin tip was orange. (Harry Gann) Below, VA-112 A-4C, BuNo 148589 NH/210, at NAS Lemoore, CA, while assigned to the USS Kitty Hawk on 10 September 1966. (Duane Kasulka) Bottom, VA-112 A-4C, BuNo 145144 NH/215, at NAS Lemoore, CA, while assigned to the USS Kitty Hawk (CVA-63) on 10 September 1966. (Doug Olson)

as part pf CVW-11.

VA-112's third A-4C deployment was to the Mediterranean aboard the USS Forrestal (CVA-59) from 24 August 1965 through 7 April 1966 as part of CVW-8. During the cruise, LTJG John C. Burch ejected just prior to his A-4C crashing through the elevator barrier and falling into the hangar deck. He did not survive the ejection and died in the ocean. Two more VA-112 pilots perished during the cruise. On 11 January 1966, LT James D. Bradford crashed at sea in BuNo 149501 AJ/501 and on 1 April 1966, LTJG Charles E. Galloway crashed off the port bow shortly after catapulting in BuNo 147840.

During training between deployments, two other aircraft were lost.

On 12 August 1966, CDR John H. Alvis in BuNo 148567 flamed-out enroute from NAS Lemoore to Dyess AFB. Unable to effect a re-start, he safely ejected from 8,000 ft. near Cannon AFB. Then, on 19 October 1966, LCDR J.C. Eichinger in BuNo 147674 collided with a VF-114 F-4B 120 miles SW of San Diego, with all three aviators ejecting safely.

Three combat deployments followed, two aboard Kitty Hawk and one aboard Ticonderoga. The first CVA-63 Vietnam cruise was from 5 November 1966 through 19 June 1967. On 20 January 1967, LTJG Jerry F. Hogan flew into the ground in BuNo 145144 NH/415 on a barge attack near Hoang Xa. Then on 27 March 1967, LT Alexander J. Palenscar failed to return from a

Above, VA-112 A-4C, BuNo 147783 NH/402, on 22 July 1967. Fin tip remained yellow instead of becoming orange on this aircraft. (Harry Gann) Bottom, Zuni-armed VA-112 A-4C, BuNo 145144 NH/415, aboard the USS Kitty Hawk off Vietnam in 1965. (USN)

bombing attack on the Dao My bridge. The following month, on 24 April, the squadron launched its planes from the USS Essex in a multi-carrier strike against Kep airfield northeast of Hanoi. The CO, CDR M.L. Minnis, Sr., was awarded the Silver Star for action during a strike against the thermal power plant at Haiphong.

The second war deployment was aboard Kitty Hawk from 18 November

1967 through 28 June 1968 as part of CVW-11. During the squadron's second War cruise, they only lost one aircraft. BuNo 148486 NH/405 was shot down by a SAM-2 while leading an Iron Hand flight near Haiphong. The pilot, LCDR Edward D. Estes, became the first POW of 1968.

VA-112's final A-4C deployment was to Vietnam aboard the USS Ticonderoga (CVA-14) from 1 February through 18 September 1969 as part of CVW-16. The carrier was pulled off line from 16 April to 10 May in response to the loss of an EC-121 to the North Koreans in the Sea of Japan. During the cruise, there were no combat losses, but two aircraft were lost operationally in July. BuNo 148310 AH/410 crashed into the sea after a failed catapult launch on 22 July 1969 with LT F.K. Helmsin safely ejecting. On 26 July 1969, LT Richard D. Brenning was killed when BuNo 147833 AH/416 crashed into the sea on another failed catapult launch.

Above, VA-112 A-4C CAG bird, BuNo 149573 NH/400, in flight in 1965 while assigned to the USS Kitty Hawk (CVA-63). (USN) Below, VA-112 A-4C, BuNo 149575 AH/414, after a wheels-up landing while assigned to CVA-14. (USN) Bottom, VA-112 A-4C, BuNo 148490 AH/407, assigned to the USS Ticonderoga (CVA-14) at NAS Lemoore, CA, on 26 October 1968. Fin tip and fuselage stripe were yellow. (Gann)

ATTACK SQUADRON ONE HUNDRED THIRTEEN, VA-113 "STINGERS"

Fighter Squadron One Hundred Thirteen (VF-113) was established on 15 July 1948 with F8F-1 Bearcats. VF-113 then flew F8F-2s, F4U-4Bs, F9F-5s, F9F-2s, F9F-8s, and finally F9F-8Bs before being redesignated Attack Squadron One Hundred Thirteen (VA-113) in March 1956. The squadron received the A4D-1 on 29 April 1957 and the A4D-2 on 8 September 1958. VA-113 upgraded to the A4D-2N (A-4C) on 29 March 1961 and received the A-4F in October 1967. The squadron transitioned to the Vought A-7B Corsair in the fall of 1968. The F/A-18A Hornet was acquired and the squadron was redesignated VFA-113 on 24 August 1983.

The squadron deployed its A-4Cs four times, three times aboard the

Above, VA-113 A-4C, BuNo 149541 NH/301, landing aboard the USS Kitty Hawk (CVA-63) in 1964. Fin tip was medium blue. (USN via Barry Miller) Below, bird farm, seven VA-113 A-4Cs, BuNos 149540 NH/311, 149541 NH/301, 147759 NH/312, 147727 NH/307, 148438 NH/306, 149495 NH/309 and 147842 NH/305, and five VA-112 A-4Cs aboard the USS Kitty Hawk (CVA-63) at Yokosuka, Japan, in October 1962. (Minoru Nomura)

USS Kitty Hawk (CVA-63) and once aboard the USS Enterprise (CVAN-65). The first CVA-63 deployment was a WestPac cruise from 13 September 1962 through 2 April 1963 as part of CVG-11. During this cruise, the Kitty Hawk's first jet centurian was a VA-113 pilot.

The second CVA-63 WestPac was from 17 October 1963 through 20 July 1964 as part of CVW-11. In June, during the cruise, VA-113 provided in flight refueling support to the Air Wing.

The third Kitty Hawk deployment was a Vietnam War cruise from 19 October 1965 through 13 June 1966 as part of CVW-11 once again. Four aircraft were lost during the cruise. The first was BuNo 148510 flown by

Above, VA-113 A-4C, BuNo 149495 NH/309, assigned to the USS Kitty Hawk (CVA-63) in 1964. (Harry Gann) Below, VA-113 A-4C, BuNo 149495 NH/303, trapping aboard CVA-63 in 1966. LTJG H.G. Welch safely ejected from this AAA damaged aircraft along the side of the carrier on 20 April 1966. (USN via Gary Verver) Bottom, VA-113 A-4C, BuNo 148472, trapping on CVA-63 in 1965-66 during its participation in the washable camouflage operational test. (USN)

LT David W. Wickham who died when he hit the round down after a combat mission on 17 December 1965. On 17 April 1966, LTJG A.E. Johnson ejected safely from BuNo 148583 after catapulting from the ship. On 20 April 1966, the CO, CDR John Abbott, was hit by AAA in BuNo 148512 NH/314 and died in captivity. LTJG H.G. Welch's A-4C, BuNo 149495 NH/303, was hit by AAA while orbiting CDR Abbott and after returning to the ship was unable to lower his landing gear. He ejected along side of the ship and was rescued safely.

Above, VA-113 A-4C, BuNo 148510 NH/309, was lost at sea when LT David Wickham hit the round down after a combat mission and was killed on 17 December 1965. (R. Harrison via Norm Taylor) Below, VA-113 A-4C, BuNo 147836, aboard CVA-63 in 1966. Aircraft armed with three Zuni pods mounted on the centerline. (Mark Aldrich collection) Bottom, VA-113 A-4C, BuNo 147723 NG/412, on 10 September 1966 with CVW-9 tail code. (Clay Jansson)

Between cruises on 19 August 1966, CDR Robert E. Bennett ejected safely from BuNo 145124 near Denver during a cross country from NAS Lemoore to Minneapolis.

The fourth deployment and second war cruise was aboard the USS Enterprise (CVAN-65) from 19 November 1966 through 6 July 1967 as part of CVW-9. On 4 May 1967, LTJG J.S. Graham became a POW when BuNo 148514 NG/314 was hit by AAA and went down over the North. On 18 May 1967, LT R.J. Haughton also became a POW when BuNo 147842 NG/316 was hit by AAA and went down.

Above, VA-113 A-4C, BuNo 147841 NG/413, at NAS Lemoore, CA, on 10 September 1966. (Duane Kasulka via Norm Taylor) Below, VA-113 A-4C, BuNo 147847 NG/301, assigned to the USS Enterprise (CVAN-65) in 1967. (Harry Gann) Bottom, VA-113 A-4C, BuNo 147734 NG/313, while assigned to CVAN-65 in 1967. Fin tip was blue. (Harry Gann)

ATTACK SQUADRON ONE TWO FIVE, VA-125 "ROUGH RAIDERS"

The Navy's second squadron designated VA-125 was established as Attack Squadron Twenty-Six on 30 June 1956 flying F9F-8B Cougars. VA-26's mission was changed to the indoctrination and training of pilots and enlisted personnel in attack aircraft for the fleet. The squadron was redesignated VA-125 on 11 April 1968, and the A4D-1 replaced the Cougars on 10 June 1958. The A4D-2 was added in August 1958 and the A4D-2N (A-4C) was added to the training syllabus on 3 March 1960. The AD-5 was added in September 1960 and the A-4E in December 1962. The TA-4F arrived on 19 May 1966 and the A-4F was acquired in February 1968. A-7 Corsairs were added in 1969 and the squadron was

disestablished on 1 October 1977 at NAS Lemoore, CA.

During its life, the squadron acquired a total of eighty-five A-4Cs as training aircraft. Of these, VA-125 lost at least sixteen while training new attack pilots. Eight pilots ejected safely. They were: LT Richard L. Grant in BuNo 147711 on 2 March 1963, LTJG Roger A. Shaffer in BuNo 145102 on 31 May 1963, LT Thomas P. Lawton Jr. in BuNo 148448 on 28 September 1965, ENS Anthony K. Vanko in BuNo 145115 on 15 October 1965, LCDR Charles Brown in BuNo 150589 on 22 November 1965, BuNo 145093 on 7 January 1968, LTJG John C. Brittenhan in BuNo 147777 on 7 March 1968, and LTJG George B. Clark in BuNo 148537 on 29 May 1969. Eight pilots

Above, VA-125 A4D-2N, BuNo 145091 NJ/541, in 1961. (Ginter collection) Bottom, VA-125 flight line in 1966 with an A-4A, A-4B, A-4Cs, A-4Es, and TA-4Fs in 1966. (Harry Gann)

were killed. They were: ENS William C. Brooks in BuNo 149554 on 10 October 1964, LTJG J.R. Frazier in BuNo 149510 on 10 October 1964, ENS Donald P. Huntley, Jr. in BuNo 149511 on 20 February 1965, LTJG Rosolino J. Territo in BuNo 147817 on 9 March 1965, LTJG Clyde E. Edgar in BuNo 147771 on 4 August 1965, LTJG Walter R. Cox in BuNo 149609 on 19 August 1966, LT Larry E. Smith in BuNo 148565 on 11 September 1968, and LTJG Victor A. Demick in BuNo 148527 on 25 June 1969.

Above, VA-125 A4D-2N/A-4C, BuNo 147706 NJ/533, armed with Bullpups on 30 May 1962 while on display at NAS Lemoore, CA. Nose and tail trim were da-glo red. (William Swisher) Below, VA-125 A-4C, BuNo 159604 NJ/555, during carrier qualifications aboard the USS Kitty Hawk (CVA-63) in 1967. (R.W. Harrison via Norm Taylor)

ATTACK SQUADRON ONE HUNDRED FORTY-FOUR, VA-144 "ROAD RUNERS"

VA-144 originally was established as VA-116 with the F7U-3M on 1 December 1955, and transitioned to the FJ-4B Fury in 1958. The squadron was redesignated VA-144 on 23 February 1959. This was a highly unusual event, as it occurred half-way through a deployment aboard the USS Ranger (CVA-61). On 4 June 1962, VA-144 received A4D-2Ns followed by A-4Es in July

1967. In 1970, The A-4F was obtained before the squadron was disestablished on 29 January 1971.

VA-144 made four WestPac deployments with their A-4Cs, three of which were to Vietnam. The first cruise was aboard the USS Constellation (CVA-64) from 21 February through 10 September 1963 as part of CVG-14.

The second CVA-64 A-4C deployment was a war cruise to Vietnam from 5 May 1964 through 1 February 1965, again with CVW-14. While conducting Yankee Team Operations over Laos, VA-144 became the first operational unit to drop Snakeyes in combat. On 4 August, VA-144 flew night sorties in support of the destroyers USS Turner Joy (DD-951) and the USS Maddox (DD-731) following their encounters with North Vietnamese Motor Torpedo Boats. During this cruise, in

response to the Tonkin Gulf Incident, on 5 August 1964 LTJG Everett Alvarez was shot down in 149578 NK/411 by AAA over North Vietnam, making him the first naval POW of the war. No other losses occurred during the cruise.

While training for the next deployment, on 16 August 1965, the squadron XO, CDR Charles H. Peters, ejected safely from BuNo 149561 66 miles south of San Diego, CA.

VA-144 was re-assigned to the USS Ticonderoga (CVA-14) from 28 September 1965 through 13 May 1966 as part of CVW-5 for its third A-4C deployment. LTJG John V.

Below, two VA-144 A-4Cs, BuNos 149553 NK/404 and 149583 NK/402, over Mt. Fuji in 1963. (Tailhook)

Above, VA-144 A-4C, BuNo 149553 NK/404, taxiis at Da Nang in September 1964 while assigned to the USS Constellation. (Tailhook) At right, VA-144 A-4C, BuNo 149561 NK/408, on CVA-64's elevator on 1 September 1964. (USN) Bottom, VA-144 A-4Cs, BuNos 147790 NF/552 and 149561 NF/542, over the Pacific on 15 August 1965. (Mark Aldrich collection)

McCormick was killed when BuNo 149560 NF/547 was shot down by AAA on 1 December 1965. On 9 February 1966, LCDR Jack L. Snyder was hit by an SA-2 missile in BuNo 149557 NF/546. He ejected safely as the aircraft broke up and was rescued. Five days later, while returning from a mission over Laos, LTJG J.C. Durham ejected over the water and was recovered after his engine quit in BuNo 149552 NF/543. A fourth aircraft, BuNo 145081 NF/553, was lost on 20 March 1966 when LTJG J.L. Pinneker was killed during a napalm attack.

The squadron's last A-4C deploy-

Above, VA-144 A-4C, BuNo 148558 NH/311, ashore in Vietnam in 1966-67 while assigned to CVA-63 and armed with a Bullpup. (Tom Hansen) At left, VA-144 A-4C, BuNo 148608 NH/303, landing aboard CVA-63 in 1967. (Lionel Paul collection) Bottom, VA-144 A-4C, BuNo 147822 NH/301, at NAS Lemoore, CA, in July 1967. Note mission marks on the engine intake. Fin tip was black and lightning bolts were red. (William Swisher)

ment was aboard the USS Kitty Hawk (CVA-63) from 5 November 1966 through 19 June 1967 as part of CVW-11. On 21 December 1966, LTJG Danny E. Glenn became a POW when he ejected from BuNo 148507 NH/303 15 miles west of Mu Ron Ma.

ATTACK SQUADRON ONE HUNDRED FORTY-SIX, VA-146 "BLUE DIAMONDS"

Attack Squadron One Hundred Forty-Six (VA-146) was established on 1 February 1956 at NAS Miramar, CA. VA-146 was originally equipped with F9F-5 Panthers and F9F-6/8 Cougars. They transitioned to the FJ-4B Fury in September 1957. On 5 June 1962, the first of fourteen A-4Cs arrived to replace the Fury Bravos. All fourteen aircraft were received in June at the squadron's new base at NAS Lemoore, CA. The squadron made four A-4C deployments before transitioning to the Vought A-7 Corsair in June 1968. On 21 July 1989, VA-146 was redesignated VFA-146 and received the F/A-18C Hornet.

VA-146's first A-4C WestPac deployment was aboard the USS Constitution (CVA-64) from 21 February through 10 September 1963 as part of CVG-14. On 8 July 1963, LTJG D.R. Gissel was killed in BuNo 149568 from injuries received when he crashed into the water three miles ahead of the ship.

The second CVA-64 A-4C deployment was a war cruise to Vietnam from 5 May 1964 through 1 February 1965, again with CVW-14. VA-146 took part in Yankee Team Operations from 8 June through 13 July 1964 and from 15 through 20 September 1964. Then, on 4 and 5 August 1964, VA-146 flew night sorties in support of Desoto Patrol operations conducted by American destroyers. Operation Pierce Arrow was conducted on 5 August, which involved retaliatory air strikes against North Vietnamese torpedo boats and their bases and support facilities for the attack against the USS Maddox (DD-731) and the USS Turner Joy (DD-951) on 4 August. No VA-146 aircraft were lost in combat, however BuNo 149570 NK/606 piloted by LTJG James H. Knollmueller was lost when he ejected safely after he collid-

ed with a VMCJ-1 RF-8A on 13 November 1964.

A second A-4C combat deployment was conducted by VA-146 aboard the USS Ranger (CVA-61) from 10 October 1965 through 25 August 1966 as part of CVW-14. On 1 February 1966, VA-146's CO, CDR Hubert B. Loheed, was lost in BuNo 149527 during a raid against barges 20 miles north of Vinh. On 5 May 1966, BuNo 149527 flew into the water, recovered, caught fire and the pilot ejected safely during an armed reconnaissance mission off the coast of North Vietnam. LT F.H. Magee ejected safely after he was hit in BuNo 149567 NK/604 by a 57mm AAA round below the cockpit on 25 June 1966 three miles NE of Vinh. Then, on 29 June 1966, CDR Schaufelberger, CO, led a 28-plane strike against Haiphong.

Below, VA-144's flight line in 1962 with twelve A-4Cs while assigned to the USS Constellation (CVA-64). BuNos 149582 NK/601, 149580 NK/602, 149575 NK/603, 149571 NK/605, 149570 NK/606, 149568 NK/607, 149567 NK/608, other five unknown. (Ginter collection)

Between deployments, LCDR John F. Kennedy was killed when he crashed BuNo 147812 20 miles SW of Fallon, NV, on 3 March 1967.

The final VA-146 A-4C deployment was a War cruise once again in CVA-64 from 29 April through 4 December 1967, again

Above, four VA-146 A-4Cs, BuNos 149559 NK/610, 149556 NK/612, 149570 NK/606, and 147839 NK/614, in flight near the USS Constellation (CVA-64) in 1964. (USN) Below, six VA-144 A-4Cs, BuNos 147812 NK/6XX, 149627 NK/6XX, NK/615, 148521 NK/604, 149556 NK/612, and 149610 NK/616, share the Ranger's deck with a VA-55 A-4E and a Phantom. (Tailhook)

with CVW-14. On 30 June 1967, AAA downed LT John M. McGrath, who became a POW, in BuNo 147712 NK/605. Then, on 9 July 1967, LT Charles R. Lee was killed when BuNo 149542 NK/602 was hit by an SA-2 missile near Haiphong. LCDR J. Caslmes crashed BuNo 147719 off the starboard bow of CVA-64 and was rescued with minor injuries on 8 August 1967. VA-146's CO, CDR Robert F. Dunn, was awarded the Silver Star for his actions on 30 September 1967 during the

Above, VA-146 A-4C, BuNo 149551 NK/604, at North Island in May 1964 while assigned to CVA-64. Tail and drop tank trim were blue. (Mark Aldrich collection) At right, VA-146 A-4C poses with a wooden prop on its refueling probe. (Tailhook) Below, VA-146 A-4C CAG bird, BuNo 149575 NK/600, at NAS Lemoore, CA, on 10 September 1967 while assigned to the USS Kitty Hawk (CVA-63). (Duane Kasulka)

ATTACK SQUADRON ONE HUNDRED FIFTY-TWO, VA-152 "MAVERICKS"

Reserve Fighter Squadron Seven Hundred Thirteen (VF-713) was called to active duty on 1 February 1951 and received F4U-4s as replacements for their F8Fs. On 4 February 1953, VF-713 was redesignated VF-152 and transitioned to F-2H-3s in October 1953. VF-152 was redesignated Attack Squadron One Hundred Fifty-Two (VA-152) on 1 August 1958. The squadron received AD-6 and AD-7 aircraft in 1959 and 1962 respectively. These were replaced with A-4Bs (19) and A-4Cs (10) in February 1968 and A-4Es in May 1969.

The eleven A-4Cs on-hand in February became six in March 1968, five in April, and finally zero in May 1968. It is not known if any of the A-4Cs were ever painted in the unit's markings. Tail code would have been "AA". The squadron made one A-4B deployment aboard the USS Forrestal (CVA-59) from 22 July 1968 through 29 April 1969, the last ever for the A-4B. The squadron also made one A-4E deployment from 5 March through 17 December 1970 aboard the USS Shangri-La (CVS-38). After the cruise, VA-152 was disestablished on 29 January 1971.

On 5 April 1968, LCDR Robert L. Elich flamed-out in BuNo 147720 near the Berkley Marina in San Francisco Bay, where he ejected safely.

Below, VA-152 A-4C, BuNo 147825, as received with no squadron markings or tail code. The aircraft was assigned to VA-152 from 14 February through 26 February 1968 before going to VA-76. Intake covers were red. (Angelo Romano collection)

ATTACK SQUADRON ONE HUNDRED FIFTY-THREE, VA-153 "BLUE TAIL FLYIES"

Reserve Fighter Squadron Eight Hundred Thirty-One (VF-831) was called to active duty on 1 February 1951 with the F9F-2. VF-831 was redesignated Fighter Squadron One Hundred Fifty-Three (VF-153) on 4 February 1953. VF-153 transitioned to F9F-6 Cougars in October 1953 and FJ-3 Furyies in March 1955. In November 1955, F9F-8s were received and in April 1956 the F9F-8B was acquired. With this aircraft, VF-153 was redesignated Attack Squadron One Hundred Fifty-Three (VA-153) on 15 December 1956. A4D-1s arrived on 12 February 1957, and A4D-2s on 27 October 1958. The

A4D-2N replaced the A4D-2s on 20 June 1961 and then transferred from NAS Moffett Field, CA, to NAS Lemoore, CA, on 21 August 1961. The A-4E arrived in January 1967 and were replaced with A-4Fs in April 1968. On 14 September 1969, VA-153 transitioned to Vought A-7As. The squadron flew Corsair IIs until its disestablishment on 30 September 1977.

While flying the A-4C, VA-153 made four WestPac deployments as part of CVW-15. The first three were aboard CVA-43 and the last aboard CVA-64. The first USS Coral Sea

Above and below, VA-153 A-4Cs over Mt. Fuji, Japan, in the spring of 1962. BuNos 145087 NL/309, 147844 NL/303, 148317 NL/306, and 148541 NL/312. Fin tips and drop tank arrows were blue. (USN)

deployment was from 12 December 1961 through 17 July 1962. On 13 February 1962, BuNo 145085 was stricken after being involved in a deck accident. Ports-of-Call for the cruise were: Honolulu, Subic Bay, Sasebo, Yokosuka, Kobe, and Hong Kong.

The second Coral Sea deploy-

ment was from 3 April through 25 November 1963.

The squadron's first combat deployment was aboard CVA-43 from 7 December 1964 through 1 November 1965. In February 1965, VA-153 participated in Yankee Team, Barrel Roll, and Steel Tiger Missions in Laos. Also in February, on the 7th and the 11th, they participated in operations Flaming Dart I and II, reprisal strikes. On the 11th, LT W,T. Majors ejected from BuNo 149572 and was rescued when his engine quit shortly after his attack run at Chanh Hoa. In March 1965, VA-153 participated in Rolling Thunder operations. On 7 April 1965, LT William M.

Roark was hit by AAA in BuNo 148317 and ejected off shore where he drowned. Two days later, LCDR Charles H. McNeil also was hit in BuNo 148841 by AAA and ejected off shore. He was rescued by an HU-16 Albatross while in rifle range of shore. The CAG, CDR Peter Mongilardi, was killed when BuNo 149574 NL/306 was hit by a 37mm shell NW of Than Hoa on 25 June 1965. On 15 July 1965, LT A.J. Bennett was rescued after BuNo 149576 NL/308 crashed at sea following his attack on Mu Ron Ma. The CO, CDR Harry E. Thomas, was killed when BuNo 148475 NL/312 was hit by AAA while in the weeds during an Iron Hand mission.

Above, VA-153 AD4-2N, BuNo 148310 NL/310, in 1961 before Blue Tail Flyies tail markings were applied. (Ginter collection) Below, three VA-153 A-4Cs, BuNos 148317 NL/305, 147844 NL/303, and NL/302, aboard the USS Coral Sea (CVA-43) in Japan in 1963. (Harry Gann) Bottom, VA-153 A-4C line on 30 October 1964 with the squadron insignia on the intakes. BuNos: 147718 NL/313, 148481, 148310, 149572, unknown, and 148306. (Harry Gann)

VA-153's last A-4C deployment was from 12 May 1966 to 3 December 1966 aboard the USS Constellation (CVA-64). On 6 July 1966, LCDR George H. Wilkins was

killed when he flew into the ground during a night mission near Vinh in BuNo 147732 NL/304. LCDR William F. Coakley in BuNo 147763 NL/314 repeated this incident on 12 September 1966. Both pilots were flying under flares when they hit the ground. Another A-4C, BuNo 148592 NL/311, piloted by LTJG Harry S.

Edwards, also flew into the ground and was killed on 20 October 1966. During the cruise, VA-153 expended more than 26 tons of bombs, rockets, missiles, flares and 20mm rounds against enemy targets.

Above, VA-146 A-4C, BuNo 149574 NL/306, being released to launch from the USS Coral Sea (CVA-43) on 24 March 1965. CVW-15 CAG, CDR Peter Mongilardi, was killed in this aircraft on 25 June 1965. (USN) Below, VA-153 A-4Cs, BuNos 147763 NL/314 and 148519 NL/312, opperate off the USS Constellation (CVA-64) on 15 August 1966. LCDR W.F. Coakley was killed in 147763 on 12 September 1966. (USN)

ATTACK SQUADRON ONE HUNDRED SEVENTY-TWO, VA-172 "BLUE BOLTS"

VA-172 was originally established on 20 August 1945 as VBF-82. They initially were equipped with F6F Hellcats, but received 24 F4U Corsairs in late September. Originally stationed at NAS Alameda, CA, the squadron transferred to NAS Quonset Point, RI, in January 1946. While at Quonset, the squadron was redesignated VF-18A on 15 November 1946. VF-18A was redesignated VF-172 on 11 August 1948 and in March 1949 they moved to NAAS Cecil Field, FL. The squadron immediately transitioned to the McDonnell FH-1 Phantom and flew it through June when the McDonnell F2H-1 Banshee was received. VF-172 became VA-172 on 1 November 1955. The squadron flew four versions of the Banshee (F2H-1, F2H-2, F2H-4, and F2H-2B) before transitioning to the A4D-1 Skyhawk in December 1957. In May 1958, A4D-2s replaced the A4D-1s and in September 1961 the A4D-2N (A-4C) replaced the A4D-2. On 15 January 1971, VA-172 was disestablished.

VA-172 made eight deployments with the A4D-2N/A-4Cs, six aboard the USS Franklin D. Roosevelt (CVA-42) and two aboard the USS Shangri-La (CVA-38). The first was a short two-week jaunt to the Caribbean from 19 November through 30 November 1961 aboard CVA-42 as part of CVG-1.

Three Mediterranean deployments followed: from 14 September 1962 through 22 April 1963, from 28 April through 22 December 1964, and from 28 June through 17 December 1965. On 20 March 1963, LTJG Gary F. Wheatley in BuNo 149589 collided with LTJG Paul Meinhardt at about

9,000 ft within sight of the ship. Both pilots were recovered safely. In May 1963, VA-172 flew missions in support of the Haitian government's defense against a rebel attack. During a night carrier training launch, LT Donald W. Malone crashed BuNo 149545 off the bow and was killed when it exploded on impact with the water. In August 1964, fighting on Cyprus with Turkish forces had VA-172 flying peacekeeping patrols.

A WestPac war cruise followed from 21 June 1966 through 21 February 1967. Four aircraft were lost during the deployment. The first pilot ejected safely from BuNo 147677 when his engine quit off the Philippines a week before the squadron's first line period began on 4 August 1966. Then, on 20 October 1966, LTJG F.R. Purrington became a POW when BuNo 147775 AB/302 was downed by AAA. The CO, CDR Bruce A. Nystrom in BuNo 145143 AB/300 and his wingman ENS P.L. Worrell in 145116 AB/304 were both

Above, VA-172 A-4C, BuNo 148555 AB/307, at NAS Cecil Field, FL, on 12 January 1962. Lightning bolt and fin tip were blue. (USN via Barry Miller) Below, VA-172 A-4C, BuNo 149566 AB/314 refuels a VFP-62 RF-8A. (USN) Bottom, VAH-10 KA-3B refuels VA-172 A-4C, BuNo 148447 AB/308, in 1965. (USN)

killed by SAMs within 30-seconds of each other on 2 December 1966 near Phuc Nhac. LCDR Edward W.

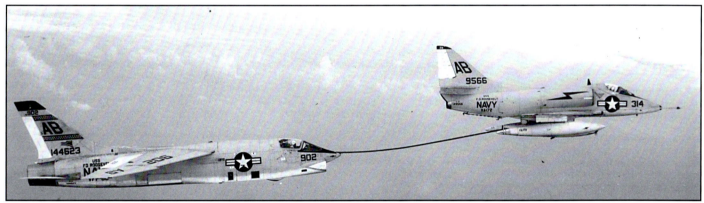

Above, VA-172 A-4C, BuNo 149537 AJ/302, landing at Atsugi in 1970. (via Harry Gann) Below, Laotian Highway Patrol insignia was yellow on black. (Weldon Dunlap) Bottom, VA-172 A-4C, BuNo 149525 AJ/313, after a divert to Da Nang in June 1970. This aircraft was lost on 23 September 1970. (Weldon Dunlap)

Oehlbeck was wounded over North Vietnam in BuNo 148608 on 18 December 1966 and landed safely at Da Nang. The aircraft was flown back to the ship on the 19th.

The Vietnam deployment was followed by another Med cruise from 24 August 1967 through 19 May 1968.

In 1969, VA-172 was reassigned to CVW-8 and the USS Shangri-La. Their first deployment was to the Med from 7 January through 29 July 1969. After this deployment, on 31 July 1969, BuNo 148441 was stricken for unknown reasons while the ship was in Mayport.

On 25 November 1969, LTJG John R. Martin in BuNo 149523 and LTJG Robert A. McLeery in 147839 collided at low level and were killed while forming-up with a third VA-172 A-4C. Portions of one aircraft crashed into a house while a second cut a firey path through the sugar pines. The third aircraft landed safely at Cecil Field.

On 10 January 1970, during flight operations aboard CVA-38, a flash fire occured while refueling a VA-72 A-4C on the forward deck. Two crewmen were severely burned, AA Stuart B. Williams and AN James E. Sexton, Jr. A third crewman, AMS-3 George Rose was treated for a fractured pelvis. All three were taken to the Jacksonville Naval Hospital where Williams later died.

VA-172's last A-4C deployment was to Vietnam from 5 March through 17 December 1970 aboard CVA-38. Target fixation claimed the life of

LTJG John B. Gotz in BuNo 148184 AJ/305 during a night attack on a truck trail near Ban Taian on 22 April 1970. On 22 June 1970, LT John S. Earls flew into the water 10 miles from the ship due to unknown causes while flying BuNo 148495. The bridle hook of BuNo 149525 failed on launch on 23 September 1970 while LTJG Hartman was flying. He was quickly rescued with minor injuries.

Above, VA-172 A-4C, BuNo 148610 AJ/306, after trapping after returning from a mission on CVA-38 in June 1970. (Barry Miller) Below, VA-172 A-4C, BuNo 147735 AJ/303, catapult shot from CVA-38 off the coast of Vietnam. (USN via Barry Miller)

VF-153 was established on 26 March 1945 with F6F-3 Hellcats. They were redesignated VF-15A on 15 November 1946 and received F8F-1 Bearcats in November 1947. On 15 July 1948, they became VF-151 and transitioned to the F8F-2 in July 1949. Then, on 15 February 1950, they became VF-192. As VF-192 the squadron flew F4U-4s, F9F-2s, F9F-5s, and F9F-6s. On 15 March 1956, VF-192 was redesignated Attack Squadron One Hundred

At top right, VA-192 A4D-2N, BuNo 145132 NM/206, landing aboard the Bon Homme Richard in 1961. (USN) At right, VA-192 A-4C, BuNo 145140 NM/207, taxis on CVA-31 on 23 July 1962. (USN) Below, VA-192 A-4C, BuNo 145140 NM/207, at NAS Lemoore in 1963. Note yellow dragon's head aft of the intake and the full dragon on the drop tank. (Ginter collection)

Ninety-Two (VA-192). In June, they received F9F-8s and F9F-8Bs. These were replaced with FJ-4B Furyies on 10 December 1957. The A4D-2 Skyhawk entered the scene in July 1959 and the A4D-2N (A-4C) arrived in June 1960. The A-4E replaced the A-4C in June 1966 and the A-4F replaced the Echos in 1967. The squadron transitioned to the Vought A-7E Corsair on 26 February 1970 and was redesignated VFA-192 on 10 January 1986. As VFA-192, the Golden Dragons flew the F/A-18A Hornet.

VA-192 made four deployments with the A-4C, all aboard the USS

Bon Homme Richard (CVA-31) as part of CVG/CVW-19. The first was a WestPac cruise from 26 April through 13 December 1961. During the cruise, on 6 June 1961, LT A.S. Falconer, while still operating from Moffett Field, CA, crashed on take-off when his engine quit and he ejected safely.

On 1 January 1962, VA-192 transferred to NAS Lemoore, CA, prior to its second WestPac deployment from 12 July 1962 through 11 February 1963.

The third deployment was a war cruise to Vietnam from 28 January

Above, VA-192 A-4C, BuNo 147681 NM/212, in flight over the Pacific in 1964. (Craig Kaston collection) Bottom, VA-192 A-4C, BuNo 145132 NM/206, in flight in 1964. Fin tip and drop tank tips were yellow. (Tailhook)

through 21 November 1964. On 15 August 1963, during weapons training for this deployment, LCDR F.M. Humphreys safely crash landed BuNo 145120 at NAAS Fallon, NV, when the engine quit due to fuel starvation. LT Ted Higgins was killed in BuNo 147699 when he crashed astern of the ship on 11 February 1964. Then, while in the Philippines

Above, VA-192 A-4C, BuNo 149920 NM/201, with Bullpups in 1965. (USN) At right, A-4C, BuNo 149606 NM/205, in 1965 with Bullpups. (USN) Bottom, VA-192 CAG-19 bird, BuNo 147683, at NAS Lemoore, CA, in 1966. Fin tip was yellow. Rudder stripes were red, green, orange, and blue. Intake chevrons were yellow, blue, orange, green, and red. (William L Swisher)

on 21 May 1964, LTJG Joe Cooke was killed when he crashed off Panay Island in BuNo 145140 NM/207. The Gulf of Tonkin incident occurred the first week in August 1964, which caused the cruise to be extended with no further losses.

A second war cruise was conducted from 21 April 1965 through 13 January 1966. The squadron only lost one plane and pilot during this war cruise. On 14 September 1965, LTJG Neil B. Taylor was killed by AAA over South Vietnam in BuNo 147682.

Torpedo Squadron Nineteen (VT-19) was established on 15 August 1943 with TBM Avengers. VT-19 was redesignated Attack Squadron Twenty A (VA-20A) on 15 November 1946 and received AD-1 Skyraiders on 3 May 1947. They became VA-195 on 24 August 1948 and flew various versions of the Skyraider until 1 July 1959, when the squadron received the A4D-2 Skyhawk. The A4D-2N arrived in May 1960 and the A-4E in September 1968. The Vought A-7E replaced the Skyhawks in February 1970 and the F/A-18A replaced the A-7Es in September 1985. VA-195 was redesignated VFA-195 on 1 April 1985 while equipped with the F/A-18 Hornet.

VA-195 made six A4D-2N/A-4C deployments as part of CVG/CVW-19: Four aboard the USS Bon Homme Richard (CVA-31) and two aboard the USS Ticonderoga (CVA-14).

The first CVA-31 deployment was

Above, VA-195 A-4C, BuNo 147710 NM/509, landing at NAS Atsugi, Japan, on 3 January 1963. Fin tip and drop tank trim were green. (Toyokazu Matsuzaki) Bottom, VA-195 A-4Cs, BuNos 147712 NM/503 and 148607 NM/505, over the Pacific in 1963. (USN)

a WestPac from 26 April through 13 December 1961. One aircraft and pilot was lost to a ramp strike during the cruise. This was LCDR Allen B. Price in BuNo 147679 on 19 July 1961. On 27 November 1961, LTJG

Thomas L. Smith Jr., died near Atsugi, Japan, when he diverted his stricken aircraft, BuNo 145137, away from the city in an effort to save lives. He ejected while too low. On return from the cruise, the squadron transferred from NAS Moffett Field, CA, to NAS Lemoore, CA.

A second WestPac deployment was made from 2 July 1962 through 11 February 1963. On 21 August 1962, Airman Apprentice Cotton died when BuNo 147692 rolled over the port side of the ship with him in it and sank. Three planes were lost on 22 September 1962 during a night refueling operation off Japan. All three pilots ejected, but LCDR John T. Parks was not recovered. Two of the aircraft were BuNos 145142 and 148542, the third

Above, VA-195 A-4C, BuNo 148603 NM/508, landing at NAS Atsugi, Japan, on 3 January 1963. (Toyokazu Matsuzaki) Below, VA-195 A-4C, BuNo 149509 NM/502, in 1964. (Ginter collection) Bottom, VA-195 A-4C, BuNo 145111 NM/510, at Edwards AFB, on 22 May 1965. (Duane Kasulka)

BuNo is not known.

Two CVA-31 war cruises followed. The first was from 28 January through 21 November 1964. In response to the Tokin Gulf Incident the first week in August 1964, VA-195 flew escort and reconnaissance sorties over North Vietnam and the Plain of Jars in Laos.

The second Vietnam War cruise was from 21 April 1965 through 13 January 1966. LTJG J.B. Worcester was killed in action on 19 October 1965 due to unknown causes in BuNo 148584 NM/512. During the deployment, the squadron flew over 2,500 combat sorties against targets in North and South Vietnam, including the Vinh Army Barracks and the Hai Duong Highway Bridge north of Hanoi.

A third war cruise was conducted aboard CVA-14 from 15 October 1966 through 29 May 1967. A ramp strike in BuNo 145123 took the life of LCDR Chester L. Nightengale, Jr., on 29 October 1966 while in route to Japan. On 13 December 1966, LTJG Donald O. Taylor ejected safely and was recovered after an attack on a SAM site near the Xuan Mai Bridge in BuNo 147776 NM/502. A second pilot, LCDR Charles E. Barnett also was rescued after being shot down by an SA-2 in BuNo 147819 NM/500 during the same raid. On 27 February 1967, LT Richard A. Luker crashed into the sea off the port bow in BuNo 148607 NM/512 and was recovered safely. CO, CDR Charles E. Hathaway, was hit by ground fire

Above, LCDR C.L. Nightengale Jr. hit the round down on CVA-14 in BuNo 145123 on 29 October 1966 and went over the side and died. (USN) Bottom, VA-195 A-4C, BuNo 149509 NM/502, makes a gear up landing into the barricade. (USN)

while strafing a truck park on 7 April 1967 in BuNo 149639 NM/506. He caught fire, but made it to the sea and ejected safely.

The final VA-195 A-4C war cruise was from 28 December 1967 through 17 August 1968 aboard Ticonderoga. No aircraft were lost during the cruise. After returning from this deployment, on 18 September 1968, LTJG Clarence K. Miles was killed when he struck high power lines in the Central Valley of California in BuNo 147689.

Above, four VA-195 A-4Cs, BuNos 147819 NM/500, 148586 NM/501, 149509 NM/502, and 149633 NM/503, dumping fuel in formation in late January 1966. (USN) Below, VA-195 A-4C, BuNo 145132 NM/509, while assigned to CVA-14 on 10 September 1966. (Duane Kasulka) Bottom, VA-195 CAG bird A-4C, BuNo 145112 NM/500, at NAS Lemoore, CA, in October 1967. (Harry Gann)

Above, VA-203 A-4L, BuNo 148538 6F/2, in 1970. (Ginter col.) Below, VA-203 A-4L CVWR-20 CAG bird, BuNo 148307 AF/300, in August 1973. (Norm Taylor) Bottom, VA-203 A-4L, BuNo 149555 AF/304, in November 1973. (Norm Taylor)

With the re-organization of the reserves on 1 July 1970, VA-203 was established at NAS Jacksonville, FL, as part of Reserve Air Wing Twenty (CVWR-20). The squadron was formed around the personnel and assets of VA2F-1 (formerly VA-741). VA-203 flew the A-4L until April 1974 when the A-7A arrived, These were replaced with A-7Bs in August 1977 and A-7Es in September 1983. On 1

October 1989, VA-203 was redesignated VFA-203. VFA-203 was disestablished on 30 June 2004.

BuNo 148578 was lost on approach to Jacksonville on 20 May 1972 with Don Condon at the controls. He was on final when his engine quit and he ejected safely low over the Ortega River. His aircraft pan-

caked on the water and came to rest upside down on the bank.

A-4Ls assigned to VA-203 were: BuNos 145077, 145092, 147671, 147703, 147750, 147780, 147825, 148307, 148505, 148538, 148578, 148586, 148600, 149497, 149531, 149551, 149555, 149556, 149594, 149633, 149635, and 150598.

ATTACK SQUADRON TWO HUNDRED FOUR, VA-204 "RIVER RATTLERS"

Above, VA-791/792 A-4C, BuNo 148533 6M/4, at NAS Memphis, TN, on 29 March 1970. (Fred Roos) Below, VA-204 A-4L CAG bird, BuNo 148611 AF/400, in 1973. Rudder stripes were: red, yellow, blue, orange, and green. (Ginter collection) Bottom, VA-204 A-4L, BuNo 149640 AF/401, at Buckley AFB in March 1971. Rudder stripes and drop tank arrow were red. (Barry Miller)

On 1 July 1970, VA-204 was established at NAS Memphis, TN, as part of Reserve Air Wing Twenty (CVWR-20). The squadron was formed around the personnel and A-4Cs of the former VA-791/792. VA-203 replaced the A-4Cs with the A-4L in August 1970. They flew it until March 1978 when the A-7B arrived, These were replaced with A-7Es in June 1986. On 1 October 1989, VA-204 was redesignated VFA-204 and received the F/A-18 Hornets. The squadron was transferred to NAS New Orleans in January 1978.

On 7 February 1971, LCDR Sid C. Dabbs ejected safely from BuNo 149579 six miles from NAS Memphis while on approach. In May 1972, VA-

204 participated in the multi-service exercise Exotic Dancer V. Then on 7 April 1974, LCDR Paul E. Burke, Jr., crash landed BuNo 149539 at the Anniston-Calhoun County Airport, AL, after his engine failed. He crashed short of the runway and skidded on fire about 250 ft. down the runway before stopping. Despite the intense flames, he unstrapped and walked away with minor injuries.

Tragedy struck the squadron on 6 March 1975 when LT Gary Carver was killed after colliding with LCDR James S. Greenwood while returning to NAS Millington. LCDR Greenwood ejected safely. BuNo 147723 was lost on 11 June 1975, when its engine blew on approach to Millington and LCDR Norris Flagler ejected safely. The squadron's last loss was BuNo 148530. LT Jerry Brett ejected safely seven miles southwest of Harrison, AR, when his plane became unfly-

able.

A-4Ls assigned to VA-204 were: BuNos 145076, 145077, 145078, 145133, 147690, 147696, 147708, 147723, 147727, 147736, 147744, 147772, 147787, 147806, 147843, 148306, 148479, 148487, 148490, 148530, 148538, 148586, 148600, 148611, 149508, 149532, 149539, 149573, 149579, 149583, 149593, 149604, 149608, 149623, 149630, 149640, and 150598.

Above, VA-204 A-4L CAG bird, BuNo 145078 AF/400, on 7 August 1975. Rudder stripes were red, yellow, blue, orange, green, black, and maroon. (Bob Mills) At right, VA-204 A-4L, BuNo 149593 AF/415, in 1976. (Ginter col.) Bottom, VA-204 A-4L, BuNo 148600, at Lambert Field, MO, on 21 August 1976. Snakes on the hump and drop tanks and rudder stripes were red. AF on tail was also highlighted in red. (Fred Roos)

ATTACK SQUADRON TWO HUNDRED FIVE, VA-205 "GREEN FALCONS"

On 1 July 1970, VA-204 was established at NAS Atlanta, GA, as part of Reserve Air Wing Twenty (CVWR-20). The squadron's first twelve A-4Ls arrived on 1 September 1970. They were flown until September 1975 when the A-7B Corsair II arrived, These were replaced with A-7Es in June 1984,

and A-6 Intruders beginning in August 1990. VA-204 was disestablished on 31 December 1994.

BuNo 148453 was lost in a mid-air collision on 20 June 1971 five miles north of Rome, GA. One pilot, LT Frederick R. Boardman, was killed but LCDR John E. Owens ejected safely from BuNo 149569. In August 1971, the three CVWR-20 A-4L

Above, VA-205 A-4L, BuNo 148498 AF/510, with Falcon on the side in 1973. (Ginter col.) Below, VA-205 A-4L, BuNo 145133 AF/504, at NAS Miramar, CA, in October 1975. (Duane Kasulka)

squadrons, VA-203, VA-204, and VA-205, spent two weeks ACDUTRA aboard the USS John F. Kennedy (CVA-67). This was the first complete

VA-205 A-4L, BuNo 148588 AF/511, in 1971. Drop tank and tail trim were green as well as the Falcon painted on the fuselage side. (Fred Roos)

Reserve Carrier Air Wing deployment aboard a carrier. On 11 November 1971, LT James E. Zerblis was killed after ejecting from his exploding A-4L, BuNo 147717, ten miles north of Baxley, GA. Then, in May 1972, VA-205 participated in the multi-service exercise Exotic Dancer V. On 15 June 1974, CDR Raymond M. Currie was killed when he crashed BuNo 148498 into the side of a mountain near Sylva. His wingman could not explain the cause of the crash.

Above, VA-205 A-4L, BuNo 147782, at Atlanta, GA, on 10 August 1974. Fin flash was green. (Bill Curry) Below, VA-205 A-4L, BuNo 147782 AF/506, at Sheppard AFB, TX, on 28 September 1974. (Bob Mills) Bottom, VA-205 A-4L, BuNo 145077 AF/511, in May 1975. Check marks, Falcon, and rudder tabs were green. (Kaston col.)

ATTACK SQUADRON TWO HUNDRED NINE, VA-209 "AIR BARONS"

With the re-organization of the reserves on 1 July 1970, VA-209 was established at NAS Glenview, IL, as part of Reserve Air Wing Twenty (CVWR-20). The squadron was formed around the personnel and assets of VA-724 and VA-725/VA-8 Air Barons in July 1968 and Detroit

At top right, VA-209 A-4L, BuNo 149623, was acquired from VA-5Y1 in 1970. Note VA-209 lance on the drop tank. (Mark Aldrich collection) Above, VA-209 A-4L, BuNo 150586 7V/51, was received from VA-8 (VA-725) at NAS Glenview, IL, on 1 August 1970. (Paul Stevens via Norm Taylor) Below, VA-209 A-4L, BuNo 147708 7Y/5, was acquired from VA-5Y1 at NAS Detroit, MI. It is seen here in September 1970. This became the Air Baron flight demonstrator AF/6, and later AF/614. (Norm Taylor collection)

based VA-5Y1. VA-209 equipped with the new A-4L and was disestablished on 15 August 1971.

The Air Barons of VA-8 were flying the A-4B in 1967 when they formed the first-and-only reserve flight demonstration team. When they were absorbed into VA-209, the Air Barons switched to the A-4L in late 1970. The team was made up of six demonstration pilots and a narrator who could double as a demonstration pilot. They operated the following seven A-4Ls: BuNos 149623 AF/1, 149506 AF/2, 149635 AF/3, 147827 AF/4, 148446 AF/5, 147669 AF/6, and 147708 AF/7. These nose numbers were later changed to 600 series numbers as assigned to the rest of the squadron. The A-4L team pilots were: narrator and CO, CDR Jim Mahoney; lead, LCDR Phil Lockard; right wing, LT Cecil Ewell; left wing, LT Dick Brent; slot, CDR Terry Denton; delta left, LCDR Don Wells; and delta right, LT Bill Underdown.

"AIR BARONS" FLIGHT DEMONSTRATION TEAM AIRCRAFT

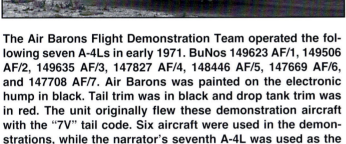

The Air Barons Flight Demonstration Team operated the following seven A-4Ls in early 1971. BuNos 149623 AF/1, 149506 AF/2, 149635 AF/3, 147827 AF/4, 148446 AF/5, 147669 AF/6, and 147708 AF/7. Air Barons was painted on the electronic hump in black. Tail trim was in black and drop tank trim was in red. The unit originally flew these demonstration aircraft with the "7V" tail code. Six aircraft were used in the demonstrations, while the narrator's seventh A-4L was used as the spare. (Ginter collection)

Above, VA-209 A-4L, BuNo 147708 AF/614, at NAS Glenview, IL, on 4 April 1971. Hump and drop tank markings were black. (Fred Roos) At left, VA-209 A-4L, BuNo 147827 AF/611, at NAS Glenview, IL, on 31 July 1971 with a full bomb load. (Art Krieger) Below, six out of seven Air Baron flight demonstration pilots pose with their aircraft and a pretty guest at Glenview in the summer of 1971. (Ginter collection)

ATTACK SQUADRON TWO HUNDRED SIXTEEN, VA-216 "BLACK DIAMONDS"

Attack Squadron Two Hundred Sixteen (VA-216) was established on 30 March 1955 with AD-4B Skyraiders. They later flew AD-5s, AD-6s, and AD-7s until being replaced with A4D-2s on 16 February 1959. These were replaced five months later with FJ-4B Furyies. On 4 September 1962, the A-4C replaced the Fury Bravo. The squadron's "C"s were exchanged for "B"s in August 1966, which were replaced with A-4Cs again beginning in February 1968. In June 1969, the A-4E replaced the A-4C. VA-216 was disestablished on 1 August 1970.

The squadron made four deployments with the A-4C, three of which

Below, flight of three VA-216 A-4Cs in 1963. BuNos: 149620 NP/607, 149622 NP/606, and 149623 NP/605. Trim was black. (USN) Bottom, flight of four VA-216 A-4Cs in 1964. BuNos: 149626 NP/683, 149606 NP/680, 149623 NP/685, and 149612 NP/690. (USN)

were war cruises to Vietnam. The first deployment was a WestPac cruise aboard the USS Hancock (CVA-19) from 7 June through 16 December 1963 as part of CVG-21.

The second Hancock deployment was again a WestPac cruise from 21 October 1964 to 29 May 1965. This turned into a war cruise after the Tonkin Gulf Incident occurred the first week in August 1964. From 29 December 1964 to May 1965, VA-216 participated in Yankee Team operations, armed reconnaissance flights over Laos, Barrel Roll operations, and armed reconnaissance and strike missions in eastern Laos. On 30 December 1964, LT Frank S. Crismon was killed in BuNo 149625 when he hit the round down on his 8th landing attempt and caught fire. VA-216 took place in Operations Flaming Dart I and II on 7 and 11 February 1965, and in Rolling Thunder Operations in March through May 1965. On 3 March 1965, LT Thomas

F. Mineau was conducting an instrument approach at night off of Manila in BuNo 149612 when he failed to return to the ship. On 3 April 1965, LCDR Raymond A. Vohden became a POW when small arms fire brought down BuNo 148557.

The squadron's third A-4C deployment was a second war cruise aboard CVA-19 from 10 November 1965 through 1 August 1966 while still with CVW-21. In March 1966, VA-216 participated in Operation Jackstay which provided close air support for amphibious operations in the river channels southeast of Saigon. On 21 May 1966, LCDR O.F. Baldwin was hit in BuNo 148473 NP/690, while attacking a cargo barge near Phong Bai. His plane caught fire, briefly, which damaged the starboard main gear making it inoperable. He ejected safely along side of CVA-19 and was recovered. A second pilot, LTJG Paul E. Galsnti, became a POW when BuNo 148528

Above, VA-216 A-4C, BuNo 149620 NP/687, assigned to the USS Hancock (CVA-19) on 30 October 1965. (William Swisher) Bottom, VA-216 A-4C, BuNo 148576 NP/681, at NAS Lemoore, CA, on 10 September 1966. Trim was black. (Duane Kasulka)

NP/693 was downed by small arms fire while hitting a rail yard at Qui Vinh on 17 June 1966. LCDR Baldwin was shot down on 4 July 1966 by AAA in BuNo 149616 NP/688. He ejected safely and was recovered. Another aircraft, BuNo 148456 NP/685, was lost on 7 July when LCDR W.J. Isenhour was struck by AAA and ejected safely. The next day, BuNo 149494 NP/683 was lost when a bomb dropped off the aircraft during the catapult shot. The pilot, LT Paul Hagland, ejected safely and was recovered.

After the 1965-1966 cruise, VA-216 re-eqipped with A-4Bs and

deployed to the Med aboard the USS Saratoga (CVA-60) from 2 May to 6 December 1967.

VA-216's last A-4C deployment was another war cruise to Vietnam from 7 September 1968 through 18 April 1969, this time aboard the USS Coral Sea (CVA-43) as part of CVW-15. A pilot, CDR Marvin J. Naschek, was killed on 21 November 1968 in BuNo 148608 when he lost altitude and crashed into the sea after his launch. Three VA-216 aircraft were lost to AAA during the cruise. The first, BuNo 147764 NL/610, was hit over Laos on 3 January 1969 during a Steel Tiger mission. The pilot, LTJG R.M. Aaron, made it to the sea near Chu Lai before ejecting and being recovered. On 14 February 1969, LTJG Larry J. Stevens was killed over Laos in BuNo 149529 NL/607 during a night interdiction mission over the Ho Chi Minh Trail with an A-6 intruder and VA-216's LCDR J.F. Meeham in BuNo 148547 NL/601. Unlike Stevens who crashed into the ground,

Above, VA-216 A-4C CAG bird, BuNo 148514 NP/00, at NAS Lemoore, CA, on 12 September 1966. Commander Carrier Air Wing Twenty-One is written on the fuselage side. (Harry Gann) Below, three VA-216 A-4Cs assigned to CVA-43 in early 1968. (Harry Gann) Bottom, VA-216 A-4C, BuNo 148603 NL/604, at Lemoore in 1969, (D. Olson)

Meeham was able to nurse his crippled aircraft out to sea near Hue where he ejected and was recovered safely.

ATTACK SQUADRON THREE HUNDRED THREE, VA-303 "GOLDEN HAWKS"

Attack Squadron Three Hundred Three (VA-303) was established at NAS Alameda, CA, on 1 July 1970 as part of Reserve Carrier Air Wing Thirty (CVWR-30). It absorbed the assets and personnel of VA-20G2 (formerly VA-876). By the end of July, fifteen A-4Cs had arrived, two more were received in August, and five more in January/February 1971. They all were replaced with A-7A Corsair IIs in April 1971, which were replaced with A-7Bs in August 1977 and F/A-18s in October 1985. VA-303 was redesignated VFA-303 on 1 January 1994 and disestablished on 31 December 1994.

Above, VA-303 A-4C, BuNo 147748 ND/310, in storage at MASDC in 1971. Fin and rudder tabs and drop tank trim were blue. (Norm Taylor collection) Below, VA-303 A-4C, BuNo 148550 ND/313, at MASDC in April 1971. (Terry Waddington via Kaston) Bottom, VA-303 A-4C, BuNo 145099 ND/302, in storage in April 1971. (Terry Waddington via Kaston)

176

ATTACK SQUADRON THREE HUNDRED FOUR, VA-304 "FIREBIRDS"

Attack Squadron Three Hundred Four (VA-304) was established at NAS Alameda, CA, on 1 July 1970 as part of Reserve Carrier Air Wing Thirty (CVWR-30). It absorbed the assets and personnel of VA-20G1 (formerly VA-879). By the end of July, thirteen A-4Cs had arrived, four more were received in August, two more in September, six more in January 1971, and one in April. They all were replaced with A-7A Corsairs in August 1971 which were replaced with A-7Bs in September 1977 and A-7Es in September 1986. In July 1988, VA-304 received the A-6 Intruder and

the F/A-18 Hornet in 1985 when they were redesignated VFA-304. The squadron was disestablished in 1994.

A-4C aircraft assigned to VA-304 were: BuNos 145100, 145111, 145118, 145125, 145129, 145132, 145139, 147687, 147761, 147845, 148311, 148467, 148513, 148525, 148526, 148528, 148529, 148610, 149493, 149500, 149506, 149522, 149540, 149577, 149626, 149642,

Above, VA-304 A-4C, BuNo 149642, at MASDC in 1971. Aircraft was only operated by VA-304 in August 1970. (Ginter collection) Below, VA-304 A-4C, BuNo 148513 ND/412, at NAS Alameda, CA, in March 1971. The tail code of CVWR-30 was this stylized "ND" seen here. (Angelo Romano collection)

and 150592.

ATTACK SQUADRON THREE HUNDRED FIVE, VA-305 "LOBOS"

VA-305 was established at NAS Los Alamitos, CA, on 1 July 1970 as part of CVWR-30. It absorbed the assets and personnel of VA-771, VA-772, VA-773 and VA-776. Shortly thereafter, the squadron moved to NAS Point Mugu, CA, as Los Alamitos was scheduled to close as a Naval Air Station on 30 June 1971. By the end of July 1970, sixteen A-

4Cs had been assigned, two more were received in January 1971, two more in February, one more in May, and one in August 1971. Seven A-4Es were acquired in January 1972 and the Vought A-7A arrived in June 1972. In 1987, VA-303 became VFA-305 and received F/A-18 Hornets. They flew the Hornets until disestablishment in December 1994. A-4Cs assigned to VA-304 were: BuNos 145114, 145121, 145127, 145128,

Above, VA-305 A-4C, BuNo 149600, in 1970. All trim was green. (Ginter) Below, VA-305 A-4C, BuNo 145128, on 15 July 1970. (Fred Roos) Bottom, VA-305 CAG bird, A-4C, BuNo 147847, in January 1971. (Clay Jansson)

147678, 147681, 147687, 147702, 147733, 147734, 147741, 147790, 147814, 147847, 148468, 148573, 148587, 149526, 149531, 149544, and 149600.

ATTACK SQUADRON EIGHT HUNDRED SEVENTY - THREE, VA-873

VA-873 was one of the Naval Reserve squadrons that were activated in response to the capture of the USS Pueblo (AGER-2) by the North Koreans on 23 January 1968. Three A-4B Skyhawk squadrons were called-up on 27 January 1968. They were VA-776 (NAS Los Alamitos), VA-831 (NAS New York), and VA-873 (NAS Alameda). Only VA-873 re-equipped with A-4Cs. Like VA-776, VA-873 wore tail code "NR" until assigned to a Carrier Air Wing. VA-873 received A-4Cs in May 1968 and was assigned to CVW-2 ("NE" tail code) on 1 July 1968. Before it could deploy, VA-873 was returned to reserve status on 12 October 1968.

Below, VA-873 CO, CDR Glen Stinnett, Jr. in BuNo 145121 taxis the deck of (CVA-19) during carrier qualifications in May 1968. (Romano collection) Middle. VA-873 A-4C, BuNo 148513, at NAS Alameda on 18 September 1968 with CVW-2 "NE" tail code. Fin tip and lightning bolt were yellow on all aircraft. (Jansson via Romano) Bottom, VA-873 A-4C, BuNo 149506, at Alameda on 18 September 1968. (Jansson via Romano)

In the 1970s through 1990s, Capt Laidlaw, president of Flight Systems Inc., operated numerous ex-military aircraft from Mojave, CA, carrying out government-sponsored test programs in ordnance, electronics, etc. Most of these were F-100s and F-4s, but he also operated one FJ-4B and a handfull of A-4C and A-4L Skyhawks.

Above, Flight Systems A-4C (N401FS) and A-4L (N403FS) bank over Mojave, CA, in 1985. (Barry Miller collection) Below, Flight Systems A-4C (N402FS) at Mojave in 1984. (Ginter)

1/72 SCALE FUJIMI DOUGLAS A-4C SKYHAWK, KIT NUMBER 25026

Fujimi 1/72 A-4C kit number 25026 was released in 1987. It was molded in 68 crisp white pieces and 4 clear parts. The kit includes a choice of five aircraft markings: VA-76 (149645 AG/301), VA-12 (149553 AJ/401), VA-144 (149561 NK/408), VA-144 (149532 NK/312), and VA-15 (148459 AA/412). The model has parts for a closed canopy or an open one and poseable slats and flaps. Three drop tanks and two Bullpups are provided as choices for the wing stores.

1/48 SCALE HASEGAWA DOUGLAS A-4C/L SKYHAWK KITS

In 2001, Hasegawa released their 1/48 scale Douglas A-4C, kit number 07222. Box art showed a Forrestal assigned VA-15 aircraft, BuNo 148543 AA/401, with its unique gold trim. Also included were decals for a VA-153 A-4C, BuNo 147825 NL/302, aboard the USS Coral Sea (CVA-43). This model is of excellent quality, save one shortcoming, no weapons. The kit only contains the two wing drop tanks. The same kit, decals and box art have been re-issued in 2019 using the same kit number 07222.

In 2003, parts were added to the basic A-4C kit and it was re-issued as a humpback A-4L. Kit number 09496 (box top not seen here) had decals for two aircraft. Box art showed an A-4L, BuNo 147754 JE/05, assigned to VC-2 in 1976. Additional decals for a VC-13 A-4L, BuNo 147825 UX/3, were also included.

Also released in 2003 was kit number 09513 (box top middle right), A-4C BuNo 149645 AG/301 assigned to VA-76 Spirits aboard the USS Independence (CVA-62).

DOUGLAS A-4C / L SKYHAWK COLORS

Above, the second A4D-2N, BuNo 145063, at Douglas in October 1958 in its colorful test paint scheme. (Harry Gann) Below, Naval Air Engineering Center (NAEC) A-4L, BuNo 149646, at NAS Lakehurst, NJ, in April 1979. (Terry Waddington) Bottom, Naval Missile Center (NMC) A-4C, BuNo 145073 NMC/87, at NAS Pt. Mugu, CA, in December 1969. (Duane Kasulka)

Above, VSF-1 Det 10 A-4C, BuNo 147710 AU/02, assigned to the USS Yorktown (CVS-10) on 31 July 1969. (William Swisher)
Below, VSF-1 CAG bird A-4C, BuNo 148356 AG/500, on the catapult of the USS Independence (CVA-62) in June 1968. (USN)

Above, Naval Aerospace Recovery Facility (NARF) NA-4C, BuNo 145063, at El Centro, CA, in 1973. (Harry Gann) Below, VC-2 A-4C, BuNo 147783 JE/3, at NAS Miramar, CA, on 26 August 1973. (Bob Lawson) Bottom, VC-7 A-4C, BuNo 147733 UH/14, in October 1972. (T. Waddington)

Above, VA-12 CAG bird A-4C, BuNo 149600 AB/400, assigned to the USS Franklin D. Roosevelt (CVA-42) for its 1967-1968 deployment. (Bob Lawson) Below, VA-12 A-4Cs, BuNos 149491 AB/401 and 149503 AB/403, aboard the USS Franklin D. Roosevelt (CVA-42) in 1964. (USN) Bottom, VC-12 A-4L, BuNo 149516 JY/3, at NAS Oceana, VA, on 25 September 1976. (Jim Sullivan)

Above, VC-13 A-4L, BuNo 147825 UX/3, at NAS Miramar, CA, on 1 May 1975. (Paul Minert collection) Below, VA-15 A-4C, 148543 AK-401, at Douglas, Long Beach, in May 1968 just prior to the squadron's CVA-59 deployment. (Harry Gann) Bottom, VA-22 A-4C, BuNo 149555 NE/201, at Edwards AFB, CA, in July 1967. (Nick Williams)

Above, VS-34 A-4C, BuNo 149593 AC/305, assigned to the USS Saratoga (CVA-60) in 1965. (Mark Aldrich collection) Below, VA-36 A-4C CAG bird, BuNo 149539 AK/500, at Long Beach, CA, while assigned to the USS Intrepid (CVS-11) in February 1969. (Harry Gann) Bottom, VA-56 A-4C, BuNo 151184, assigned to the USS Enterprise (CVAN-65) on 28 December 1967. (William Swisher)

Above, VA-64 A-4C, BuNo 147733 AG/610, while assigned to the USS Independence (CVA-62). (Harry Gann) Below, VA-66 A-4C, BuNo 145122. (Clay Jansson) Bottom, VA-76 A-4C, BuNo 148314 NP/681, at NAS Lemoore, CA, while assigned to the USS Bon Homme Richard (CVA-31). (Harry Gann)

Above, VT-86 A-4C, BuNo 145097 4B/18, at NAS Glynco, GA, on 8 October 1973. (Fred Roos) Below, VA-93 A-4C, BuNo 147710 NG/310, while assigned to the USS Enterprise (CVAN-65). (Harry Gann) Bottom, VA-94 A-4C, BuNo 149531 NG/412, at NAS Lemoore, CA, on 21 August 1965 while assigned to the USS Enterprise (CVAN-65). (William Swisher)

Above, VA-95 A-4C, BuNo 149508, assigned to the USS John F. Kennedy (CVA-67) at NAS Alameda, CA, on 2 January 1969. (William Swisher) Below, VA-106 A-4C, BuNo 148546 AK/309, poses with its possible weapons. (Nick Williams collection) Bottom, VA-112 A-4C, BuNo 145144, at NAS Lemoore, CA, while assigned to the USS Kitty Hawk on 10 September 1966. (Doug Olson)

Above, VA-113 A-4C, BuNo 147715, in April 1966. (Craig Kaston collection) Below, VA-153 A-4C, BuNo 147825 NL/302, while assigned to the USS Coral Sea (CVA-43). (Harry Gann) Bottom, VA-192 CAG-19 bird, BuNo 147683, at NAS Lemoore, CA, in 1966. (William L Swisher)